Vision Critical Studies

General Editor: Anne Smith

Scott Fitzgerald:
Crisis in an American Identity

SCOTT FITZGERALD:
CRISIS IN AN
AMERICAN IDENTITY

Thomas J. Stavola

VISION

Vision Press Limited
11–14 Stanhope Mews West
London SW7 5RD

ISBN 0 85478 174 9

Printed in Great Britain
by Clarke, Doble & Brendon Ltd
Plymouth and London
MCMLXXIX

To Roberta

There are all kinds of love in the world, but never the same love twice.

Scott Fitzgerald

Contents

Acknowledgments

One of the singular pleasures of writing a book is that it gives the author an opportunity to thank certain people for their help and support during the course of its stages. I wish to acknowledge my intellectual debt to the late Marius Bewley. This study of Scott Fitzgerald began under his inspiring direction. I am grateful to John Antush and Vincent Blehl, S.J., for the active interest they have taken in my work. I wish to thank Robert Kloss and Joseph Salerno who kindly read the manuscript of this book and offered many helpful suggestions. I am also indebted to Ellen Rose and Carol Perazzo for providing me with useful insights. My thanks must be expressed to Mary Kirkegard for her thoughtful and meticulous assistance in the preparation of the manuscript.

I am especially grateful to John Becker whose generous help and encouragement have been truly invaluable. I would also like to thank the students in all the courses I have taught both at Fairleigh Dickinson University and The New School for Social Research. Their ideas, reactions and, most of all, loyalty have influenced me greatly.

Finally, my deepest gratitude, beyond words, is to the person to whom this book is dedicated.

* * *

Grateful acknowledgment is made to the following for permission to reprint previously published material:

Brandt and Brandt: Excerpts from *Zelda: A Biography* by Nancy Milford. Copyright © 1970 by Nancy Wilson Milford. (Harper and Row, Publishers, Inc.)

Houghton Mifflin Company and William Heinemann Ltd.: Excerpts from *The Far Side of Paradise* by Arthur Mizener. Copyright © 1965 by Arthur Mizener.

W. W. Norton and Company, Inc. and Faber and Faber Ltd.: Excerpts from *Identity: Youth and Crisis* by Erik H. Erikson. Copyright © 1968 by W. W. Norton and Company, Inc.

Harold Ober Associates, Inc.: Excerpts from the writings of F. Scott Fitzgerald as they appear in *Scott Fitzgerald* by Andrew Turnbull, *The Far Side of Paradise* by Arthur Mizener, and *Zelda: A Biography* by Nancy Milford. Also excerpts from the writings of Zelda Fitzgerald as they appear in *Zelda: A Biography* by Nancy Milford. All rights reserved and protected as stated herein.

Charles Scribner's Sons and the Bodley Head: Excerpts from F. Scott Fitzgerald's *The Beautiful and Damned* (Copyright © 1922 Charles Scribner's Sons); *The Great Gatsby* (Copyright © 1925 Charles Scribner's Sons); *Tender is the Night* (Copyright © 1933 Charles Scribner's Sons); *This Side of Paradise* (Copyright © 1920 Charles Scribner's Sons); *The Letters of F. Scott Fitzgerald*, edited by Andrew Turnbull (Copyright © 1963 Frances Scott Fitzgerald Lanahan); and excerpts from *Scott Fitzgerald* by Andrew Turnbull (Copyright © 1962 Andrew Turnbull).

Introduction

During the past seventy-five years radical changes in almost every aspect of modern life have caused a generally recognized unsettling of the sense of American cultural identity. Among the most significant writers of the twentieth century who have struggled with the complex dimensions of this problem, as well as offered a tolerable solution, is Scott Fitzgerald. He did this so memorably in his works because his own life was so persistent a search for identity. The subject of his best writing was always his own "transmuted biography". It is well documented that Fitzgerald wrote almost exclusively about his own divided nature, the achievements and hopes of the confident, romantic young man who was also fearful of himself and the world. This struggle was further complicated by his relation to American culture. Fitzgerald was constantly tormented by the conflict between the seduction of the American Dream and his belief in the value of the traditional virtues of "honor, courtesy, and courage".

Any psychoanalytic theory capable of illuminating the life and works of Fitzgerald must address both the struggles of the individual and the context of these struggles, the larger culture. Since Erik Erikson believes that the process of human development is located in the interaction of the individual with his communal culture, his theory provides a most useful means of relating the identity crisis of Fitzgerald and those of the major male characters in his four completed novels to American culture. The main ingredient of that culture might be defined as a naïve but not deterministic belief in the limitless material promises of American life. A product of the Frontier rather than of Puritanism, this belief in the goodness of man and nature rejects all forms of deprivation. The limitless space and boundless resources of the American land have been turned, here, into a psychological naïveté about the possibilities of the individual self. The tendency is to forget that youth passes and the body weakens. Similarly, the sense of history

11

and the traditional values that have been affirmed in the ordered life of other societies is pushed aside in the hope of being able to escape the moral boundaries assumed by those values.

Erikson furnishes the ideal conceptual tools for studying both Fitzgerald's individual struggles and the problem of American cultural identity. At the centre of Erikson's ego-psychology is his concept of psychohistory as set forth in his reluctantly designed system of eight stages of development, each stage characterized by psychic polarities which account for the ambiguities of life. The fifth stage, when an adolescent usually pursues the formation of an identity, is critical in the development of an integrated personality. Erikson has described the often misused term identity as an awareness of continuity in the style by which the self tests and acquires new capacities and roles, a style that also coincides with the continuity in one's meaning for significant others in the immediate community. Identity, according to Erikson, is a life-long process, never really complete or free from redefinition. It takes shape from previous identifications and from a growing capacity for fidelity in relationships and in work. This forms the necessary basis for the accomplishments of maturity: intimacy and generativity, a responsible care for the next generation.

But psychoanalysis without a social dimension would be less than adequate as a critical tool for dealing with the artist hero of a generation. Erikson's psychohistorical writings on Luther, Gandhi, Jefferson, Shaw and such fictional characters as Emanuel Borg, the hero of Ingmar Bergman's *Wild Strawberries*, combine psychoanalytic insight with a creative historical imagination. These are not narrow case histories that represent a rigid application of his scheme of the human life cycle to the lives of major historical leaders, artists, and fictional characters. Rather they reflect as well Erikson's firm grasp of the social, political, and cultural history of the individual's environment. It is for this reason that the psychosocial relativity at the heart of Erikson's theory makes his insights valuable tools for investigating and understanding more accurately the American identity crises of Fitzgerald and his major male characters.

1

Erik Erikson's Human Life Cycle

Erik Erikson proudly professes that Freudian analytic theory is the "rock" on which he has founded his investigations and the structure within which he has articulated his insights into the personality. But no matter how stubbornly Erikson insists on his debt to Freud, there is little doubt that during his long career he has moved far beyond the Freudian model of the person in the basic psychoanalytic formulations he assumes his readers understand and accept.

Erikson believes that every individual possesses a life cycle consisting of eight developmental stages that expand according to the epigenetic principle. Somewhat generalized, this inner law, as Erikson explains, "states that anything that grows has a ground plan, and that out of this ground plan the parts arise, each part having its time of special ascendancy, until all parts have arisen to form a functioning whole".[1] The epigenetic growth of humans, however, is presented by Erikson in terms of inner and outer "crises". The word *crisis* is used here in a developmental sense to connote not a threat or a condition of imminent disaster, but a necessary turning point, a crucial moment of heightened vulnerability and potential when human development must move one way or another. Therefore, in each stage of life's development, every individual must confront and master an essential and dominant issue which appears in the form of an often painful dilemma. Erikson uses the word "versus" (vs.) to describe the vital struggle that exists between the alternative basic attitudes of each of the eight stages: (1) trust vs. mistrust; (2) autonomy vs. shame; (3) initiative vs. guilt; (4) industry vs. inferiority; (5) identity vs. identity confusion; (6) intimacy vs. isolation; (7) generativity vs. stagnation; and (8) integrity vs. despair.

All of Erikson's stages are basically related in several fundamental ways. Each possesses its own unique developmental theme while playing a part in the previous and subsequent stages and in the complete plan of development. Unlike Freud, Erikson stresses the state of continual movement in each stage. A person therefore never possesses a completely finished personality or identity or sense of any basic virtue such as trust. He is always resynthesizing or refining any one or all of these stages. The crisis of the sense of basic trust vs. mistrust is not totally resolved during a child's first year or so of life. It may emerge at each consecutive stage of development with good or ill effects. A child who is filled with a sense of basic mistrust because of a seriously impaired early relationship with his mother may, at a later time, come to trust himself through another adult who provides the time and authentic psychological motivation. Also, a child who possesses a vibrant sense of trust from his early days may have an equally strong sense of mistrust ignited later if a painful rupture occurs in a relationship with an emotionally significant adult.

Although Erikson establishes an average timetable for the ego's progress through the stages of life, a person successfully moves on to the next stage only when he is biologically, psychologically, and socially prepared and ready. For a person must derive from each stage a specific vital strength and from all the stages an epigenetic system of such strengths which create human vitality. Erikson calls these strengths basic virtues because he believes that without them all other values and goodnesses lack vitality. His justification for the use of the word "virtue" is that it once suggested the meaning of an inherent strength: a medicine or a drink was said to be "without virtue" when it had lost its power. In this sense Erikson uses the term "vital virtue" to connote certain qualities which begin to animate man pervasively during successive stages of his life.

Erikson also claims that each person possesses a generational principle which tends to perpetuate this series of vital virtues throughout his life cycle and that of his children. As identified by Erikson, the vital virtues are conceptualized as follows: Hope, in infancy; Will and Purpose, both in the play age; Skill in the school age; Fidelity, in youth; Love, in young adulthood; Care, in adulthood; Wisdom, in old age.

A human being, as Erikson is always very careful to stress, is "at all times an organism, an ego, and a member of a society and is involved in all three processes of organization."[2] This strong emphasis upon the influences and processes of socialization is represented in each stage by a relevant social institution. Organized religion is the institution that throughout time has rigorously attempted to verify a person's basic trust which then becomes the capacity for faith. This is a vital need since man appears compelled to find in some social institution a tangible formula that will adequately explain and defend him from evil.

The first five stages of Erikson's life cycle include infancy, childhood, and adolescence. The last three fall within adulthood. But Erikson has discussed the first (trust vs. mistrust) and the fifth (identity vs. role confusion) more thoroughly than the other six because of their significance for our almost obsessive contemporary preoccupation with proper child-rearing techniques and the power of youth. Similar to the oral stage of orthodox psychoanalytic theory that lasts about fifteen months, Erikson places the foundation for all ensuing human development during the first stage. In his view the child's earliest social experiences, especially with the mother and father, are the sources of his pervasive attitude towards himself, other people and the world which becomes one of either basic trust or mistrust. By trust Erikson means "an essential trustfulness of others as well as a fundamental sense of one's own trustworthiness".[3] This also implies that the young child must learn to trust the unknown, the unpredictable, and even his own sense of mistrust. Essentially the amount of trust derived from early infantile experiences depends upon the quality of the maternal relationship because, as Erikson concludes, "Mothers create a sense of trust in their children by that kind of administration which in its quality combines sensitive care of the baby's individual needs and a firm sense of personal trustworthiness within the trusted framework of their community's life style".[4] This in turn depends upon the strength of the mother's and father's separate identities and the quality of their interpersonal relationship. If these elements are essentially strong and healthy, the parents' union will be able to represent to the child a deep, almost somatic belief that there is a basic meaning to what they are doing.

When the parents do not possess or seek a joint philosophy of life with all its mysteries and uncertainties, the atmosphere surrounding a child breeds mistrust, suspicion, fear and apathy. Most children tend to sense the unconscious insecurities and intentions as well as the conscious thoughts and overt behaviour of their parents, even though they do not understand their cause and meaning. Therefore only a trustworthy environment can maintain a child's overall confident balance and willingness to accept the new experiences that produce psychological growth and the basis in him for a sense of authentic identity.

Erikson's second stage deals with the second and third years of infantile life. Bolstered by a growing sense of trust, the child discovers his behaviour is his own, asserts a sense of autonomy and realizes that he possesses a will. He takes pride in new accomplishments but at the same time he still remains partially dependent upon his parents. This state of ambivalence generates a sense of doubt. The child wonders whether he possesses the capacity and freedom to assert his autonomy and eventually reach independence. To this doubt is added a certain shame about his instinctive rebellion against his formerly enjoyed dependence and a fear of what exists beyond his environmental limits. These conflicting urges embody the major crisis of the second stage and once again the parents' treatment of the growing child is pivotal. During the second stage the child needs sympathetic guidance and graduated support from the parents in order that there may slowly emerge within the child a sense of mastery over himself, his body, impulses, and surroundings—a sense of autonomy. But, if the parents are impatient, overprotective, or consistently do for the child what he has the ability to do himself, a sense of fundamental self-doubt and self-shame begins to grow and fester.

During the third stage of the life cycle, the genital, the child of four or five engages in many new activities involving the body, language, and fantasy, all of which show clear signs of independence. He no longer merely responds to the actions of others; now he himself initiates different activities. But simultaneously with this further maturity is the emergence of the powerful governor of initiative, the conscience. This "inner" voice of self-observation, self-guidance, and self-torment, the "cornerstone of morality", is formed by the quality of the parents' superegos and their sociocultural heritage. If the child's vital activities are inhibited or overburdened by morally over-eager adults, this conscience can become constricting, cruel, and resentful, especially if the parents themselves do not live up to the conscience they have fostered in

16

the child. Conscience to him then becomes a matter of arbitrary power and not one of essential goodness. Morality then usually becomes synonymous with vindictiveness, censorship, and suppression of others. The third stage is also significant for its Oedipal complications. Erikson accepts this Freudian concept but warns about its oversimplification or misinterpretation. He affirms the existence of an attachment between the child and the parent of the opposite sex. But this reaching out is not incestuous in terms of our Western mores, rather it proves the fact that love usually extends itself to someone who is proven and readily obtainable.

Erikson states that the psychosocial dimension that emerges during the fourth stage of the life cycle is manifest in the polarity of industry vs. inferiority with the successful resolution of this crisis producing the virtue of competence. On one side there is the child's increasing concern with the nature, workings, and power of things and the fundamental skills demanded by his culture. Opposing this sense of industry is the constant pull towards a former degree of lesser accomplishment that reminds him that he is still a child. Once again the parents' relationship with the child can enhance this sense of industry by encouraging and rewarding his efforts or fuel his feelings of inferiority by ignoring or making little of his work tasks. At the same time the parents' influence lessens as friends, and especially their parents, enter a child's life. They cause comparisons to be made and oftentimes a child's parents are found lacking in certain areas.

When a person moves into the identity stage, the most complex and painful of the life cycle, he encounters a series of crucial problems and changes. These centre around a decisive interpersonal polarity, identity and role confusion. Erikson describes the psychosocial experience, identity, as an awareness of continuity in the style by which the self, usually adolescent, tests and acquires new capacities and roles, a style that coincides with the continuity in one's meaning for significant others in the immediate community whose support an individual needs for his or her development. Just as trust was necessary for an infant to grow amid new childhood experiences, so is the possession of a sense of authentic identity the foundation for making adult decisions in the areas of love and vocation.

During the period of identity formation, the adolescent develops new ways of perceiving reality. He becomes a philosopher, a theorist, "an impatient idealist". In his mind and emotions he tends to construct ideal beliefs, persons, families, and societies which seem to him as easy to find or accomplish as to fantasize about but, unfortunately, they usually fade away when exposed to the light of real life. After such disillusionment what essentially remains for the adolescent is a very serious task of personal and social integration based upon deep self-searching and clear self-diagnosis. Dating back to the first stage of life he must gather and examine everything he has learned about himself as a son, worker, student, friend, lover, success, failure living under particular defining sociocultural conditions. The result of this painful, lengthy, incomplete process is a sense of psychosocial identity provided that he has not begun with a virulent sense of mistrust, shame, doubt, guilt, or inferiority. If this last is the case, the adolescent experiences a sense of identity confusion—a serious lack of direction allied with debilitating feelings of personal dislocation and alienation.

Erikson has further defined the period of identity crisis as a time of self-standardization in the search for romantic and occupational identity.[5] If this confusing process drags on without some clarification, the adolescent, rather than remain a nobody, often tries to resolve abruptly this painful problem by selecting a "negative identity", which usually opposes the wishes of society. This form of identity, as Erikson explains, is "perversely based on all identifications and roles which, at critical stages of development, had been presented to them as most undesirable or dangerous and yet also as most real."[6]

In his analysis of identity formation, Erikson also recognizes a psychosocial safety device labelled a "psychosocial moratorium". This is a form of delay of adult commitments, such as apprenticeship, extended formal education, military draft, internship, which society formally sanctions. It is more precisely a "period that is characterized by a selective permissiveness on the part of society and of provocative playfulness on the part of youth, and yet it also often leads to deep, if often transitory, commitment on the part of youth, and ends in a more or less ceremonial confirmation of commitment on the part of society".[7] During a moratorium an adolescent usually experiences acute developmental crises in one or all of the following areas: intimacy, work, and time. He must work out his bisexual conflicts and learn to see himself

18

primarily as male or female, not part of each, if he is to move toward the fuller sense of identity which is required for intimacy and
generativity. For "True 'engagement' with others is the result and
the test of firm self-delineation."[8] If this identification fails to
grow, the adolescent experiences a tense inner reservation, caution
in commitment, or enters stereotyped fusions that amount to
mutual narcissistic mirroring, loss of existing identity, and, sometimes, isolation.

One of the major demands of identity development is an integrated and persistent commitment to a choice of occupation. The
uncertainty and anxiety involved in this task disturbs most young
people to such a degree that it creates an acute upset in the sense
of industry and the resulting patterns of workmanship, especially
if there have been faulty identifications during the school age with
parents, teachers, or other significant adults as workers. An adolescent finds it almost impossible to concentrate on any task, required
or suggested, or he may have to struggle to even begin or complete
his efforts. His diffusion of work identity may even manifest itself
in an almost self-destructive preoccupation with some one-sided
activity such as excessive physical or mental labours. This condition does not necessarily signify a lack of talent or ability for
some of the most gifted suffer from it most extremely.

During the identity crisis a youth also examines his society
and culture for a world view that will anchor his life as well as
evoke from him the virtue of fidelity, the ability to sustain freely
pledged loyalties to some set of durable values or a person who
"stands for" a meaningful ideology. The impetus to search out an
ideology or an individual is rooted in an adolescent's wish to settle
the larger framework of his life so he can devote himself to such
tasks as intimacy which he believes is an easier accomplishment.

Unfortunately, classical psychoanalysis has very little of significance to say about true intimacy. For Erikson it is only possible
when individual identity formation is well on its way. He defines
this most valuable form of relationship as a true "counterpointing
as well as fusing of identities".[9] But such intimacy, according to
Erikson, should not be taken in the narrow sense of a sexual rapport because these experiences often precede the capacity to love
or are not absolutely necessary to devlop "a true and mutual
psychosocial intimacy with another person, be it in friendship, in
erotic encounters, or in joint inspiration".[10] Oftentimes before

such intimate maturity is reached, much of a person's love life is of the self-seeking, identity-hungry kind. In reality he is trying to reach himself.

When an individual finds he cannot establish authentic intimate relationships with his own inner resources and then with others, he may settle for highly stereotyped relationships that spawn a deep isolation. This condition may be severely painful since it often creates a deep character problem for a person whom society believes is "successful" while he himself never can actually feel himself so. Intimacy, when properly achieved, produces love, a mutuality of devotion that seeks to overcome the antagonisms inherent in any close relationship between two mature adults. Marriage as a social institution sanctions one of man's deepest commitments to mutual intimacy. This way of life in Erikson's view ideally signifies the capacity and readiness of two people to share mutual trusts, to regulate the cycles of birth, work, and recreation for each others' fulfilment and then the ethical development of offspring and society.

Middle age is a time when a mature man's desire to be needed becomes stronger and more expansive. What Erikson means by the crisis of generativity is an older person's concern not only with his own family but with society and the future of mankind. Using a healthy marriage as a base a person pursues with his mate a course of action aimed at securing for the next generation the wisdom he possesses.

Where generativity fails there results a state of self-absorption or stagnation. The person becomes obsessed exclusively with his own needs and comforts. Such self-indulgence leads to interpersonal impoverishment, boredom, disgust, and a loss of a sense of caring. Thus a supposed experienced and wise man refuses to acknowledge the new generation as his responsibility and denies it the trust so basic to Erikson's first stage. In particular he refuses to support and vitalize social institutions and traditions such as child care, education, the arts and sciences, that will surely influence the life of a newly developing child.

The last Eriksonian stage presents an adult with the opportunity to evaluate his whole life cycle and finally accept the ultimate fact that one's life is one's own responsibility. Subsequently there emerges a sense of integrity whose attributes include personal dignity, satisfaction with the progress of life, and comradeship with the men and women of history. But if a person looks back upon his life as a series of extreme failures, missed opportunities, and bitter hostilities, the result is despair since time has run out. Oftentimes behind an elderly person's façade of chronic disgust and contempt for particular people and institutions hides the individual's contempt for his immature self and his fear of death.

The virtue of the eighth stage is wisdom, a detached concern with life in the face of death itself. Only the rare person can cultivate this wisdom for himself. Most seek out a vital tradition to fulfil this need. There are a variety of significant philosophical and religious systems dating back to classical times that attempt to answer a man's "ultimate concerns" with some clarity and solace. Thus each man must face a new edition of an identity crisis at the very end of his life. But his last satisfaction can be the thought that his children will not fear life, if he possesses integrity enough not to fear death.

No discussion of Erikson's human life cycle would be complete without mention of his influence upon psychohistory. Erikson's writings have clearly indicated how Freud's teachings, developed in the twentieth century, can make historical events and persons more intelligible. In his major book-length studies of Martin Luther and of Gandhi, Erikson assumes a "disciplined subjectivity" and tries to take his subject's point of view of himself and his world. He also carefully examines the significance of a particular event or crisis in the individual's life which seemed to unify the elements of his past life and motivated his future achievements. From this focal point Erikson, a gifted artist who painted children's portraits as a young man, proceeds to fill in the social and historical background. The final effect is a verbal portrait that represents not just a series of facts but a justifiable explanation of the personal and social motivations behind them. Working on the borderland both of psychology and history and of neurosis and creativity, Erikson's biographical studies are books on identity and ideology. The words, deeds and identity crisis of a struggling Luther, for example, became representative in the sixteenth century of sweeping ideological changes. Multitudes of people were drawn to the personal conflicts of an alienated monk. In this way he inspired the German nation to move towards the Protestant Reformation. Erikson therefore argues that only when an historical person like Luther deeply understands and experiences both himself and his historical actuality can he "speak to the condition" of his times. Only then do his inner conflicts and struggle become characteristic of so many vital and earnest people.

Erikson's writings in psychohistory suggest the valuable possibilities of psychoanalytic theory when used by a subtle and brilliant analyst who has thoroughly mastered history. It provides an opportunity to connect the past with the present, to compare their ethical strivings and solutions with those of today. But, most of all, at its best, such history taking advantage of Erikson's finest insights into the human life cycle engenders public and private awareness, which is no small accomplishment.

NOTES

1 Erik H. Erikson, *Identity: Youth and Crisis* (New York: Norton, 1968), p. 92.
2 Erik H. Erikson, *Childhood and Society* (New York: Norton, 1963), p. 36.
3 Erikson, *Identity*, p. 96.
4 Erikson, *Identity*, p. 103.
5 Erikson, *Identity*, p. 132.
6 Erikson, *Identity*, p. 174.
7 Erikson, *Identity*, p. 157.
8 Erikson, *Identity*, p. 167.
9 Erikson, *Identity*, p. 135.
10 Erikson, *Identity*, p. 135.

2
Scott and Zelda Fitzgerald: A Joint Psychohistorical Study

During the years since his death Scott Fitzgerald has been transformed into a "semi-divine personality" by an idolizing public that has often praised him, his life style, and his work for everything but literary reasons. This mythologizing is not difficult to trace or understand. In a country hungry for uninhibited heroes, the leading exemplar and spokesman of the Jazz Age long before his death invited his legendary status through his highly public personal life and highly personal publications.

When Fitzgerald told Maxwell Perkins, his editor at Scribner's, "I can not disassociate a man from his work",[1] he likely had himself in mind; one cannot come to critical terms with Fitzgerald's writings without a thorough knowledge of the major facts of his biography. Fitzgerald's genuine subject was a "transmuted biography", he always "wrote about himself or about people and things with which he was intimate."[2] But his writings are so effective only because he maintained a tension between his energetic wish for intimacy and hero-worship and his faculty to analyse himself and his world dispassionately in the traditional terms of good and evil.

In the study of any writer there are three concentric areas of evaluation: the man, his writings, and his society. With Fitzgerald at the centre of these areas were four major figures, Philip Francis McQuillan, his grandfather; Mollie McQuillan, his mother; Edward Fitzgerald, his father; and Zelda Sayre, his wife.

Philip McQuillan's life, like that of his author grandson, was relatively short, forty-three years. But, according to the obituaries it was "a living romance, for in the brief period of twenty years [McQuillan] passed, by his own unaided exertions, from the humblest beginnings to a place among the merchant princes of the country".[3] His Horatio Alger success story was the outstanding social and economic fact in Fitzgerald's background as well as the basic source of "vitality" in Scott's life. Unfortunately, this vital influence was transmitted by a romantic but obviously neurotic and unhappy woman, Mollie McQuillan, Fitzgerald's mother. Only after her death in 1936 could Fitzgerald in some way resolve his painfully hostile relationship with her. At that time the tragedy of his mother's life came over him in a rush; he realized that although he seemed to have had nothing in common with her except a "relentless stubborn quality", she, more than his father, was the source of his vitality and creativity.

The emotional state of Scott's mother during his birth and early infancy is fundamental to an understanding of Fitzgerald's later life. It is a time when the foundations of identity are laid with the accomplishment of a sense of basic trust, the healthy effect of the child's initial encounter with the world in the person of his mother. But if the mutuality is radically impaired by the mother's responses, the infant is left with an abiding sense of mistrust, a disruption of his relation with himself and his world.[4]

At the time of Scott's birth Mollie Fitzgerald was very unhappy. An extremely romantic but unattractive woman—her contemporaries referred to her as "witchlike"—she often found that reality fell far short of her dreams. This, in fact, was the case with her marriage of six years to Edward Fitzgerald. Mollie had entered into it out of desperation. She was almost thirty and no one else was interested in her. Scott Fitzgerald's father did not choose; he was chosen. Although he was quite good-looking, dressed well, and possessed "breeding" as well as a Southern sense of graciousness, he lacked vitality and aggressiveness. Moreover, there lingered in him an indolence or fatigue that rendered him unadaptable to the vigorous life style of the Midwest. Edward Fitzgerald was cut out for financial failure. While this was not altogether apparent when he married Mollie McQuillan, it was evident to his wife at the time of his son's birth.

Shortly before her delivery Mollie, already a disillusioned wife, suffered a period of intense grief over the death of their two previous children, both girls. Although she kept her sorrow completely within herself and never mentioned these children again, Scott eventually was to feel the branding effect of these deaths, and the "spoiled priest" in him linked them with his vocation as an artist. "Three months before I was born," he wrote, "my mother lost her other two children and I think that came first of all though I don't know how it worked exactly. I think I started then to be a writer."[5] An emotionally deprived mother and wife now poured all her affections, hopes, and fears upon her very vulnerable son. She spoiled Scott in every way possible, catering to his smallest whim. His only taste of discipline came from his father and aunts. As Scott grew older, his mother became increasingly overprotective and eccentric. Mollie constantly worried that he would succumb to a family history of tuberculosis. Henry Dan Piper describes Fitzgerald as a child "so bundled up in hats, coats, and overshoes that he developed a lifelong hatred of protective clothing of any kind. And, on the pretext of his delicate health, Mollie let him stay home from school whenever he felt like it—which was often. She also encouraged his tendency to show off in public. Nothing pleased her better than to have her five-year-old son perform for the neighbors in the front parlor, reciting poems he had memorized or singing popular ballads."[6]

Such a relationship with his mother weakened an imaginative and precocious boy like Fitzgerald. He interpreted his mother's emotional largesse as a sign of his own personal inadequacy and fragility. Fitzgerald as an infant was not allowed to develop a fundamental sense of his own trustworthiness. In addition to this Scott's trust in others was quickly shattered by the expectation that everyone would treat him as "graciously" as his mother did. Since most obviously did not, he experienced deeper feelings of mistrust and the beginnings of an ambivalent sense of hostility towards his parents, especially the mother, that pervaded his life and became a recurrent theme in his life and fiction. Moreover, this infantile sense of mistrust also extended into the area of the supernatural where it coloured his image of God and capacity for faith in an ordered universe.

Fitzgerald was reared as a Catholic. His mother was the more devout of his parents. Occasionally she joined her two spinster sisters who went off to daily Mass dressed in black with prayer books under their arms. Next to her family Mollie Fitzgerald's chief preoccupation was religion. She accepted without reservation Catholicism's habitual emphasis upon the damning effects of sin, especially sexual sin, and the existence of a legalist God who decides the moment of a person's death and his eternal fate according to rigorous norms of good and evil.

As a young boy Scott Fitzgerald was rarely more than an observing Catholic. He found his religious training strict, drab, and oftentimes, very frightening. The source of Fitzgerald's short story "Absolution" was his own childhood. At the age of eleven he told a lie in confession and suffered several days of intense horror before returning to the priest. Many years later he still remembered it distinctly as having been "a very chilling experience". Although the young Fitzgerald was attracted to certain clergymen, like Monsignor Fay and Father Joe Barron, he renounced the formal aspects of Catholicism when he entered Princeton claiming he was less than an agnostic in belief. But no matter how hard Fitzgerald tried throughout his life to turn his Catholicism into a memory, his basic feeling for experience remained a religious one. He consistently viewed life, especially his own, as a dramatic conflict between good and evil although he occasionally renounced these categories in favour of what appealed to his own aesthetic imagination.

Ernest Boyd, a friend of Fitzgerald, shrewdly said of him in 1923: "There are still venial and mortal sins in his calendar, and . . . his Catholic heaven is not so far away that he can be misled into mistaking the shoddy dreams of a radical millennium as a substitute for Paradise. . . . His confessions, if he ever writes any, will make the reader envy his transgressions, for they will be permeated by the conviction of sin, which is much happier than the conviction that the way to Utopia is paved with adultery."[7] Near the end of his life Fitzgerald wrote his daughter, Scottie: "Again let me repeat that if you start any kind of career following the footsteps of Cole Porter and Rodgers and Hart, it might be an excellent try. Sometimes I wish I had gone along with that gang, but I guess I am too much a moralist at heart, and really want to preach at people in some acceptable form rather than to entertain them."[8]

There is little doubt that Fitzgerald's early training in Catholicism played a formative role in shaping his moral judgments and selecting the various problems he struggled with in his writings: the meaning of God, love, death, good and evil, the workings of guilt, personal responsibility. Yet most critics have not involved themselves with what Henry Piper labels "the prickly question of Fitzgerald's 'Catholicism' ",[9] or they have tried to balance the negative quality of Fitzgerald's early education at various Catholic schools with his attraction to various members of the clergy. No doubt these experiences had their effects upon the young imaginative author but they are not the ultimate forces behind his unique religious temper because, as Erikson maintains, "only a reasonably coherent world provides the faith which is transmitted by the mothers to the infants in a way conducive to the vital strength of *hope*",[10] the real basis of the faith for which man must find some confirmation in a lasting religious institution. But, first of all, this hope must be nourished by the adult faith which pervades a mother's patterns of care for the child.

Fitzgerald's initial encounter with the world in the person of his God-fearing mother, as we have seen, engendered in him a prevalence of mistrust of self and others, especially his mother. Close upon the heels of these feelings and effects of insecurity Fitzgerald grew resentful of his mother and of her ambivalence towards the God of Catholicism and towards her husband. She feared and literally complied with the commands of a God who was secretly thought of as the silent cause of the deaths of her two children. She acted out her spiteful distaste for her passive husband through a constant stream of humiliating words and acts. Since the male child learns in the most profound sense of the word what it is to be a man through his perception of the father, Fitzgerald believed that to be male was necessarily to be like his father, inferior and powerless before a dominating woman. Moreover, as time went by Fitzgerald's resentment towards his mother turned to open hostility. It must have seemed to him that she had caused his crippling doubts about his manhood by depriving him of a strong identifiable father figure.

Even as a child Fitzgerald tried to release his pent-up bitterness towards his parents by claiming he was not their son. He went about the neighbourhood telling people he "had been found on the Fitzgerald doorstep one cold morning wrapped in a blanket to which was pinned a paper bearing on it the regal name of 'Stuart' ".[11] This was just one early manifestation of Fitzgerald's determination to escape from the morose world of his parents into the more exciting one of the imagination. He was convinced that the latter was far better morally and aesthetically, a friendly place where he could realize his own romantic dreams. This belief endured until 1922. While planning his third novel, *The Great Gatsby*, Fitzgerald began to seriously question the true value of his accomplishments: money, fame, and marriage to a beautiful woman.

By denying any natural bond with his parents the young Fitzgerald gained some temporary relief from the oppressiveness of his childhood. But such a resentful rejection was also guilt-inducing. No one depreciates his parents, especially his mother, no matter how unjustly they treat a child, without automatically experiencing strong feelings of guilt. In Fitzgerald's case this reaction was compounded by his early religious training which made it very clear that God was on his parents' side. They were the supreme representatives on earth of a wrathful Father who possessed the ultimate weapon of retaliation, death. By rebelling against his parents Fitzgerald was sentencing himself to a life of conflict and anguish. Guilt feelings that evoke a need for punishment would always be present along with the constant fear of death and God. These forces constantly struggled with the romantic idealism that urged him to participate in life without counting the cost. Occasionally, when Fitzgerald's enthusiastic quest would fail, the event would then take on the aspect of a terrifying reminder of his wickedness and vulnerability.

Still, for Fitzgerald, to accept the Catholicism of his parents was a fundamental fact of self-betrayal and weakness that was even more degrading because of his feelings of mistrust about himself. It meant giving up his hope of realizing his adolescent dreams of success: money, fame, a beautiful woman. It also meant pleasing his parents, especially his mother, too much. For Fitzgerald to do this was to become submissive to his mother, a carbon copy of his father, and gratify someone who had early sown the seeds of emotional upheaval in his life.

The "prickly question" of his Catholicism obsessed Fitzgerald as an adolescent. Finally when he decided to be a professional writer he noted in his ledger opposite September 1917, "last year as a Catholic". After this Fitzgerald ceased almost all external observations such as attending Mass, still he could not eliminate his innate attraction to various forms of organized religion. But his periodic ventures into religious observance were short-lived and riddled with conflict since satisfying religious practice demands a trustful, childlike surrender to a Supreme Being. Fitzgerald's capacity for such an experience, as we have seen, was severely impaired because of the negative quality of his maternal relationship.

Although his life became a quest to remedy this deprivation, the emotional void was always painfully present; so also were its ensuing conflicts with himself, his parents, God, lovers, writing, the world.

Fortunately, Fitzgerald was at his creative best when he was struggling with contradictory forces, especially the conflict in his nature between the romantic young man, confident of his ability and of the goodness of the world, and the "spoiled priest" whose vision was forever darkened by mistrust. Mizener writes that Fitzgerald's "best work is a product of the tension between these two sides of his nature, of his ability to hold in balance the impulses 'to achieve and to enjoy, to be prodigal and open-hearted and yet ambitious and wise, to be strong and self-controlled, yet to miss nothing—to do and yet to symbolize' ".[12] Not until 1936 did he lose faith in his own ability to realize this dream in his own personal life. But Fitzgerald never lost his conviction that "the test of a first-rate intelligence is the ability to hold two opposed ideas in the mind at the same time, and still retain the ability to function".[13]

Fitzgerald's mind owes its vitality and penetration to his divided nature. His best writings were imaginative attempts to close and heal this rift. Oftentimes he felt he had failed. But "a relentless stubborn quality", vitality, the only thing Fitzgerald consciously believed he had in common with his mother, drove him on in spite of himself. As he matured, Fitzgerald's judgment of his father changed. His image became "a kind of moral touchstone". Such was not the case with his mother. Fitzgerald could never completely understand or forgive her. Nor could he ever forget the "witchlike" old lady who smothered him with affection.

Scott Fitzgerald was four and living in Buffalo, New York, when the Sayres' sixth child was born on 24 July 1900, at their home on South Street. Her mother, Minnie, an avid reader, named her baby Zelda after a gypsy queen in a novel. Both the Sayres and Machens, Minnie's family, were Southerners with Victorian manners only slightly diminished. But the relationships within the Sayre nuclear family were more emotionally tangled than most. The marriage of Minnie Machen, "the Wild Lily of the Cumberland", and Judge Anthony Sayre, as Nancy Milford explains, "must have been an attraction of opposites".[14] The wife loved life intensely. She was the artist who read voraciously, wrote poetry, and dreamed of becoming an actress. Her husband was reserved and considered, by most acquaintances, a sober and dignified man who was married to his law practice. This attachment consumed almost all his waking hours. During the little time he spent with his family he continued to play his role as a judge imposing rigid Victorian standards whenever he thought discipline necessary. Because this was the only active part he played in the Sayre household his children were left with the image of a severe yet secretive man and father. Judge Sayre was reliable but certainly not a father who would evoke trust and loving identification.

When Zelda, the Sayres' last child, was born, Judge Sayre was forty-two; Minnie was nearly forty and undoubtedly knew Zelda would be her last child. At this time the four surviving Sayre children were all manifesting strong traits of independence. Since her role as a wife rarely afforded her any emotional fulfilment, this deeply disturbed their mother. In addition Minnie stubbornly refused to involve herself in the social life of Montgomery on the grounds that she was not a native. More likely, it was because her neighbours found her a bit odd or "artistic".[15] So Minnie Sayre, like Mollie Fitzgerald, showered her new child with attention and praise. She clung so tenaciously to Zelda that she nursed her until she was four years old. Threatened by the independence of her other children Minnie seemed to look upon Zelda as her last opportunity to hold onto her only clearly defined social role. Also behind Minnie Sayre's unusually close relationship with Zelda was her habit of seeing herself and the life she could have had relived through Zelda. An aborted stage career, an unsatisfying marriage, an insecure middle-age, and social isolation surely left Minnie with little trust in herself as a woman. She tried to overcompensate for her feelings of inadequacy by smothering Zelda with affection, quickly excusing her faults, and allowing her every possible freedom. But paradoxically for Zelda as for Scott, the effect of all this excessive affection was that she developed a weak sense of trust in herself.

The psychological damage done in this early period of Zelda's life occasioned behaviour later in life that was to do her irreparable harm. For no matter how many male admirers surrounded her, how many doctors treated her, how many prayers for help she sent up to a God whom she finally sought out as a last resort, Zelda could not free herself from this infantile curse of mistrust of herself and others. She continually struggled against it, however, with a relentless determination, both as a defiant youth in the Victorian world of Montgomery, Alabama, and later as a tortured mental patient constantly in and out of various hospitals.

The origin of Zelda's determination may be understood in terms of the dynamics of Erikson's second stage, autonomy vs. self-doubt and shame, which Freud has designated as the anal phase. At this stage the matter of mutual regulation between adult and child faces its severest test. The mother has supposedly stopped nursing the child who slowly assumes control of his various bodily functions and begins to test his will against the demands of others, especially the mother. This whole stage becomes "a battle for autonomy". During this time, however, Minnie Sayre was continuing to nurse Zelda, preventing her from experiencing the independence attached to learning how to feed herself as well as from the ensuing experience of a sense of self-esteem. This prolonged period of nursing, along with Zelda's initial sense of self-mistrust, stunted her nascent feelings of autonomy and engendered in her the shame and self-doubt which are the "dynamic counterpart" of the positive psychosocial achievements of the anal stage. Such feelings of inadequacy quickly emerge when a child is not allowed to perform at her own pace those small yet important acts she knows she can do at that time. If such a state of parental overcontrol continues, the child experiences a pervasive sense of powerlessness that often surfaces as acts of aggressiveness directed against herself, the parents, or anyone who in some way treats her like a helpless child.

Such responses were evident in Zelda's adult personality and behaviour, especially during those later years when she was struggling with mental illness. Burdened by insecurity and a lack of self-esteem, she often overcompensated by projecting a confident, almost defiant air of superiority that transcended all accepted laws of society. Milford rightfully describes Zelda as "an elusive woman. She was also vulnerable and willful and in deep hiding".[16]

In order to convince others of this superiority, Zelda first had to convince or delude herself. Apparently she succeeded quite well both early in life and during the years after her marriage when she sought an identity through artistic activities separate from her husband. When asked to describe herself as a little girl Zelda said "I had great confidence in myself, even to the extent of walking by myself against life as it was then. I did not have a single feeling of inferiority, or shyness, or doubt and no moral principles."[17] Such an unusual childhood, in the South of the early twentieth century seems most improbable, especially within the emotionally unhealthy context of the Sayre family. In her middle years Zelda was equally wilful about her endeavours in the areas of dancing, writing, and painting. She undertook these activities with a proud determination which oftentimes ran counter to her husband's opinion. "It was impossible for him to share her conviction that she would one day become a dancer of the first rank."[18] Scott was right about Zelda's dancing ability. Unfortunately he failed to understand the roots of her neurotic need to be independent and succeed on her own.

Yet he possessed almost the same illusion of superiority and the same driving ambition based, like Zelda's, upon his early parental relationships. Overprotectiveness, under various forms, continued for many years beyond Scott's anal period. Since a firmly developed early trust as well as an environment that backs up a child's wish to "stand on his own feet" are necessary for the growth of autonomy, Fitzgerald's insecurity was deepend by feelings of doubt in himself and doubt in the firm perceptions of his parents. At a very early age he, like Zelda, tried to neutralize these anxieties by public acts of overcompensation. He became a precocious exhibitionist who enjoyed making people believe he was a rascal, a child prodigy, an élitist snob.

Fitzgerald, as a child, was already living "with a great dream" he was determined to realize. Part of the dream was being an heroic leader wherever he went. Unfortunately, as Mizener points out, "he had a hard time understanding that other children did not exist simply as material for his uses and when they asserted their own egos with the brutal directness of children, he was always unprepared for it and deeply wounded".[19] Still he wilfully continued his escapades and tried to enjoy people talking about them. Fitzgerald, like Zelda, projected the image of owing society nothing; and when anyone made a demand of him, he usually overcame his pains of insecurity and did the opposite.

Among the repertoire of shock tactics Scott seemed to use the most was pretending he was drunk while riding on the street-car. (He actually began to drink when he was fifteen.) This ritual was more than a favourite act for the flamboyant Fitzgerald, if it is placed in the context of his flawed relationship with his father. Scott, like any son, wanted to identify with his father in some strongly masculine way. Since Edward Fitzgerald drank heavily because of his consistent failures and frustrations, his son chose drinking, a symbol of masculinity, as a form of identification. At first Scott's choice was gratifying; eventually it became a source of self-destructiveness. Ironically his father's failures were more productive than drinking. They sharpened Scott's determination to be a success.

When Fitzgerald was one-and-a-half years old, his father's business failed. The family was forced to move from Buffalo to Syracuse. This was the first of a series of employment failures and relocations that ended in 1908 when Edward Fitzgerald was fired from Proctor and Gamble. After this failure he drifted. In effect, he lived off his wife's rich St. Paul relatives. For Scott this dismissal in 1908 was traumatic. Almost twenty years later he remembered the incident this way,

> One afternoon the telephone rang and my mother answered it. I didn't understand what she said but I felt that disaster had come to us. My mother, a little while before, had given me a quarter to go swimming. I gave the money back to her. I knew something terrible had happened and I thought she could not spare the money now.
>
> Then I began to pray, "Dear God," I prayed, "please don't let us go to the poorhouse." A little while later my father came home. I had been right. He had lost his job.
>
> That morning he had gone out a comparatively young man, a man full of strength, full of confidence. He came home that evening an old man, a completely broken man. He had lost his essential drive, his immaculateness of purpose. He was a failure the rest of his days.[20]

This experience was both a serious blow and a stimulus for Fitzgerald, who loved his sensitive father. Early in life he felt that he had replaced his father as the man in the family; great things were now surely expected of him, one of which was to make allowances for his inadequate parent. Fitzgerald's change of attitude towards his father is typical of the reaction of certain types of "leading individuals". There is, as Erikson believes, "an early assumption of moral responsibility for a parent—a responsibility which they subsequently [extend] to mankind itself".[21] Yet this was still a heavy psychological burden for Fitzgerald to carry, no matter how precocious he was. Co-existing with this newly recognized will to success and the new sense of family responsibility were the equally forceful feelings of doubt and shame that challenge the development of an authentic sense of autonomy. One serious danger of such a conflict is the emergence of a "precocious conscience" which does not allow a person to get away with anything. Habitually doubtful and ashamed, he overcompensates and manifests a defiant kind of autonomy. Such was the case with Fitzgerald. He early developed a conscience that drove him to frequent displays of an "inordinate vanity". But this covering was brittle, any form of criticism could easily break through to his weak inner core, nor was he unaware of this painful vulnerability. In *The Romantic Egotist* Fitzgerald later related an honest account of himself as he was about to enter Newman prep school:

> *First:* Physically—I marked myself handsome; of great athletic *possibilities*, and an extremely good dancer. . . . Socially . . . I was convinced that I had personality, charm, magnetism, poise, and the ability to dominate others . . . Morally—I thought I was rather worse than most boys due to latent unscrupulousness and the desire to influence people in some way, even for evil. I knew I was rather cold, capable of being cruel, lacked a sense of honor and was mordantly selfish. *Second:* Psychologically—Much as I influenced others, I was by no means the "Captain of My Fate". . . . I was liable to be swept off my poise into a timid stupidity. I knew I was "fresh" and not popular with older boys . . . *Third:* Generally—I knew that at bottom I lacked the essentials. At the least crisis, I knew I had no real courage, perseverance or self-respect.
>
> So you see I looked at myself in two ways. There seemed to have been a conspiracy to spoil me and all my inordinate vanity was absorbed from that. All this was on the surface, however, and liable to be toppled over at one blow by an unpleasant remark or a missed tackle; and underneath it, came my own sense of lack of courage and stability.[22]

So ambivalent a self-image is not unexpected nor should the causes of this condition be restricted to the problems Erikson locates at the second stage of development. The successful resolution of the overlapping crisis of the third stage, initiative vs. guilt, is closely connected to a person's ability to be trusting and autonomous. Out of this must emerge a sense of initiative as a basis for a realistic sense of ambition and purpose. A child is now asked to be responsible for himself and his world. He realizes that he is looked upon as a person whose life has a purpose, and he acts upon these feelings. Oftentimes when his behaviour is unusually intrusive or restricted, he experiences the discomfort of guilt.

The latter possibility was realized for Fitzgerald as well as for Zelda. During this time the over-solicitous attitude of his mother continued with the same intensity resulting now in a frustration of his attempts to achieve a sense of initiative, along with feelings of guilt that overburdened an already precocious conscience. Moreover "where mothers dominate households the boy can develop a sense of inadequacy because he learns at this stage that while he can do well outside in play and work, he will never boss the house, his mother, or his older sisters".[23]

Once again Fitzgerald fought against the effects of this further weakening of his self-image by overcompensating. He began to want nothing less than perfection from himself because he was obsessed with the belief that in order to be loved and successful, he must be perfect. Until late in life this principle motivated Fitzgerald's behaviour especially when someone challenged him or seemed to recognize his basic weaknesses. Such a person became an enemy who must be conquered. This reaction was not just another defence mechanism for Fitzgerald; it became a source of hope that such victories would prove his superiority and eventually erase his feelings of inadequacy. As his later periods of emotional exhaustion attest, his hope was not realized.

Nor could Fitzgerald ever substantially alter the early pattern of interpersonal relationships formed by his failure to resolve his Oedipal complex, the most far-reaching complication within Erikson's third stage. Fitzgerald's ambiguous relationships with women, especially Zelda, prove that he was never able to successfully shift his basic identification from mother to father. As a young boy Fitzgerald could not relinquish his romantic attachment to his mother for two reasons. He never feared retribution from an assertive father, nor did his unhappily married mother discourage this. In fact, she nurtured, as we have seen, their deeply neurotic bond. Fitzgerald's Oedipal failure deprived him of the substantial ego strength to be derived from a strong male model and increased the sense of inadequacy that was always a controlling force in his behaviour. The tone of the self-evaluation Fitzgerald made a few years before his death is not unexpected.

I'm so bad, such a lousy son-of-a-bitch that I've got to do something so good—so good in my work—that it counterbalances the bad. I've *got* to be good and I *can* be in my work.

"I must be loved," he often mused. "I tip heavily to be loved. I have so many faults that I must be approved of in other ways."[24]

Zelda, like Scott, never resolved her Oedipal relationship. Living with an unattractive mother and a mostly unresponsive, often absent father, she grew up basically insecure and sought out ways, often socially unacceptable or destructive, to strengthen her self-image and appeal. The effects of such an unhealthy domestic situation upon Zelda were singularly deep and pervasive. Because of the strained relationship with an inaccessible father, she had little clear understanding of what a father and husband should be. Since her pleasant experiences with him were so few, she fashioned a partially fantasized idea of him which became the basic pattern of her future heterosexual relationships. At the same time Zelda was reluctantly drawn to an eccentric mother who had deliberately isolated herself from society.

Children, when confronted with the problems of an Oedipal struggle, look for new identifications which seem to promise a field of initiative with less of the conflict and guilt which are attached to the hopeless rivalry of the home. Play offers one such therapeutic outlet where boys and girls find different means for solving the conflicting drives of this phase. Zelda loved sports, especially imaginative, active, competitive games. Even the most basic exercises of roller-skating, she performed with passion and purpose in full view of anyone who looked her way. Stories about her escapades and outrageous pranks abounded in Montgomery. "For her part," Milford points out, "even as a child Zelda was not unaware of the effect she created. She possessed early a certain command over others, making them do what she wanted them to. She also had a knack of drawing attention to herself."[25] This need for an audience foreshadowed her grotesque antics during her marriage, although many of these latter were also a form of retaliation against her husband.

Zelda's early competitive spirit was later translated into her attitudes towards men, money, and status in American society. She firmly believed that to be the best she had to have an ever-growing string of young men pursuing her. This meant she had to be exceptional, mysterious, and very seductive because for a Montgomery belle with Zelda's aspirations marriage was the only means of changing the scope of her life. Marriage was the door to money, clothes, and a life of extravagant experiences in New York and Europe. Scott Fitzgerald admired Zelda's unwillingness to give up her bright dreams. In 1919 when she refused to marry him he wrote, "the girl really worth having won't wait for anybody".

Only after Scribner's accepted *This Side of Paradise* for publication and Zelda was convinced that Scott's future was bright, did she consent to marriage. Although it was not immediately apparent, Zelda chose a husband whose character was in certain ways like her father's. But the similarities between these two men did not provide a basis for friendship. They never really cared for one another. In 1931 Scott Fitzgerald knelt beside the Judge's deathbed and pleaded for some final sign of approval: " 'Tell me you believe in me.' 'Scott,' the judge had answered, 'I think you will always pay your bills.' "[26] Judge Sayre was clearly mistaken. Fitzgerald suspiciously managed to keep himself deeply in debt throughout most of his adult life. Although he had a great capacity for work, it only extended to the select areas of writing and society.

The crisis of Erikson's fourth stage, industry vs. inferiority, usually occurs during the early school years, a time of serious social maturation when the new and structured world of formal education compels a youngster to find a place among children of approximately his own age. This experience should not be shocking or essentially unsettling if the parents have performed their basic duties so as to prepare their child for school life. If not, he may discover, as Scott partially did, that his pre-school training and accomplishments do not really amount to anything substantial in the eyes of his teachers or peers. The immediate results are a further weakening of self-esteem. Moreover, a young person's untapped potential, if not properly evoked by at least one inspiring and dedicated teacher, may remain dormant, or evolve late or never.

Although Fitzgerald was consciously critical of his teachers at St. Paul's Academy, Newman, and Princeton, he still managed to seek out many authentic intellectual guides: C. N. B. Wheeler, Elizabeth Magoffin, Father Fay, Shane Leslie, Dean Gauss, Edmund Wilson, and John Peale Bishop. Fitzgerald sincerely respected them. In return they were most willing to help him, each in his own scholarly or artistic way, because they were perceptive enough to see the unique talent that Fitzgerald often concealed behind his bravado. Largely through their support he had no great difficulty arriving at an occupational identity, that of a professional writer.

From his early days at St. Paul's Academy Fitzgerald had an intense desire to write which he fell back on at Newman and Princeton when he realized that his mediocre talents in sports would not gain him the wide notoriety he craved. He learned "that if you weren't able to function in action you might at least be able to tell about it, because you felt the same intensity—it was a back door way out of facing reality".[27] Fitzgerald's early work suffered from a merely sporadic discipline, but he fully realized that writing would be a decisive means of coping with inferiority and the inability to establish identity at other levels of life. Then writing became the test and the means of satisfaction for the intense perfectionistic drive he expressed so clearly in a remark he made to Edmund Wilson shortly after leaving Princeton. "I want to be one of the greatest writers who ever lived, don't you?"[28]

In reality Fitzgerald's formal education was primarily a series of social events devised by his mother and himself to promote his personal success. Although Mollie Fitzgerald was excluded from St. Paul society because of her eccentricity and awkward mannerisms, she saw to it that her son became involved with the most prominent of his peers. In 1909 Scott entered dancing class at Ramaley Hall, where the children of the wealthiest came in black limousines, with monograms and coats-of-arms on the doors, driven by liveried chauffeurs. This dancing class typified the struggle for popularity which went on in other forms all over St. Paul and always aroused Fitzgerald's competitive sense. Throughout his life and especially during his early years of schooling and writing Fitzgerald was extremely conscious of his peers. They were decisive forces in establishing his identity, the means whereby he could gain the social importance which his family lacked.

As a teenager, however, Fitzgerald was found unacceptable by most of his peers. He possessed a pseudo-sophistication they oftentimes found strange and unpredictable. Although Fitzgerald had an ability to entertain his schoolmates, he still was not popular. He was a mixer but still clearly withheld a part of himself because he lacked a genuine trust in himself and others. Girls sought him out, but Fitzgerald would let the attention and flattery go to his head, and soon each one would tire of him.

At the St. Paul Academy, an English teacher remembered him as "a sunny light-haired boy full of enthusiasm who fully forsesaw his course in life even in his schoolboy days. . . . I helped him by encouraging his urge to write adventures. It was also his best work, he did not shine in his other subjects. He was inventive in all playlets we had and marked his course by his pieces for delivery before the school. . . . He wasn't popular with his schoolmates. He saw through them too much and wrote about it. . . . It was his pride in his literary work that put him in his real bent."[29] Early in his development Fitzgerald channelled his imagination and sense of industry into his writing. This was his first serious effort to move away from the psychic limitations imposed by an insufficient solution of previous conflicts. Opposing this, however, was the ever present pull to be the baby at home rather than the young adolescent in school, the baby who tried to hide his weaknesses by constantly exhibiting before others his own superiority without any thought of the social consequences.

While at Newman he vigorously attempted to excel in sports, especially football, but without much success. Still he was not basically discouraged. Throughout this intense and stormy quest for recognition Scott showed an unspoken bravado, some cocky assurance about his destiny, which stood between him and his fellows, most of whom had no idea where they were going. He had an ease and courtesy that were well beyond his years, having apparently skipped that awkward stage most boys must painfully go through. Considering such precocious social development it is easy to see why Fitzgerald decided to attend Princeton where men were "slender and keen and romantic" and where the atmosphere was that of a first-rate country club. Such an environment was safer for the sensitive and cerebral Fitzgerald, who lacked "animal magnetism", than Yale, where the male ideal stressed the "brawny, brutal and powerful".

From his first day at Princeton Fitzgerald naturally placed an inordinate amount of importance upon social position. He was no scholar although in other ways college life excited him. He naturally liked the big-time competition for power and status. At first Fitzgerald cautiously remained on the outskirts of the student groups conforming but also studying different clubs and individuals very carefully. He kept lists of all the clubs, their numbers, and the qualities they valued. He spied out the collegiate leaders as opposed to the "scuts" or "birds", as the lower orders were labelled. He tried to imitate the successful Princeton man, taking note of everything in such a person's conduct, even of how he treated his parents on visiting days.

When the time was ripe for Fitzgerald to advance himself socially, he became a user, a manipulator. He felt a strong attraction for the more durable rewards of life, yet he was seduced by the surface glitter of membership in a prestigious club or the title of President of the Triangle Club or a seat on the Senior Council. Naturally these activities took priority over his studies, and his grades suffered badly. Ultimately this neglect prevented Fitzgerald from realizing his social dreams at Princeton. His failures, however, did not cripple him because he was writing and publishing with great success. Nor did he have any doubts about his talents and future as a professional writer. Moreover, Fitzgerald now sought out authentic intellectuals like John Peale Bishop and Edmund Wilson, who helped him develop through their honest friendship and criticism. If the young Fitzgerald experienced any true identity confusion in the area of his career as a writer, it was unusually short-lived. When in trouble he could always rely upon his great capacity for toil which never deserted him for long.

Zelda Sayre, like Scott, found that formal schooling did not live up to her dreams or expectations. It restricted her freedom, something she rarely tolerated. Also the antics and skills that impressed her family and friends quickly established for Zelda "a reputation for cheekiness" among her peers or teachers. The school system which existed in Alabama at that time advocated a constant attention to learning and strict adherence to rules. In that type of atmosphere where school discipline was far more rigid than anything Zelda imagined her father would try to administer, most of her studies seemed valueless. For Zelda life had to be filled with occasions for overcompensating antics before an admiring audience. Unfortunately, school, especially Sidney Lanier High School, was not the best place to satisfy these needs.

Although Zelda was an above average student with a keen interest in English and mathematics, she often complained that school work was tiresome and dull, and therefore only deserving of the slightest attention. This excuse was partly valid, but Zelda was also terrified of public failure and, more importantly, of its effects upon her own self-image. To compensate for this fear she cultivated an attitude of absolute fearlessness and superiority. Most people accepted these two character traits as authentic, which led to unsatisfactory relationships between Zelda and her peer group, as well as many adults. They generally considered her eccentric like her mother and, at the worst, spoke of her as careless or immoral. To compound the problem, as Zelda matured, girls her age became envious of her way of life and attractiveness to men. This further separated them from her and from those deep friendships with peers which are essential for self-esteem. Nor was she unaware of the cause of this isolation. Subconsciously Zelda wished it were different, but to allow anyone to come close would have included the revelation of her true, insecure, and frightened self. To avoid such a risk she continued to cultivate a false image.

School for Zelda was mostly a matter of marking time. Her lack of interest was obvious even in small details like her daily dress. Although "Zelda was on the verge of becoming the most spectacular belle Montgomery would ever know",[30] experiences of her school years had many negative effects upon her future behaviour. The distance she had established between herself and most people diminished the possibility of any future intimacy. Her negative pattern of relating to others was allowed to grow and continue into her later years of courtship and marriage. Before Zelda's first breakdown she deliberately provoked extreme distaste among her and Scott's friends. During her various hospital confinements Zelda's attempts at communication with her husband, doctors or other patients seemed destined to end in failure and painful frustration.

These school years also formed Zelda's early adult attitude toward the value of work. She never considered work very important until she felt threatened. When she felt emotionally sterile or when Scott began to ignore her for his writing, much like Judge Sayre, or when she desperately sought out an identity apart from her husband, only then, like Scott, did she work, sometimes irrationally to the point of collapse. Such was the case with her ballet lessons before her first breakdown and with her painting and writing while hospitalized in various sanitaria.

Work, for the youthful Zelda, was basically for others to do, especially those like her husband who had to pay the price of her expensive life style. Scott's writing was merely the source of the cheques in the mail that bought her beautiful clothes, irresponsible all-night parties, long European vacations, and the attentions of famous people. Throughout their relationship Scott had to work both for his dream and for Zelda's survival. Whatever work Zelda did, her dancing, painting later in her life, or writing, was to prove her creativity and independence to herself and to Scott. To a much lesser extent it was also a means of therapy or pure recreation.

Fitzgerald summarized his wife's attitude toward work as well as life and love quite well in a letter to his daughter written on 7 July 1938.

> When I was your age I lived with a great dream. The dream grew and I learned how to speak of it and make people listen. Then the dream divided one day when I decided to marry your mother after all, even though I knew she was spoiled and meant no good to me. I was very sorry immediately I had married her but, being patient in those days, made the best of it and got to love her in another way. You came along and for a long time we made quite a lot of happiness out of our lives. But I was a man divided—she wanted me to work too much for *her* and not enough for my dream. She realized too late that work was dignity, and the only dignity, and tried to atone for it by working herself, but it was too late and she broke and is broken forever.[31]

Freud has said that to live well one must be able to "love and work". Erikson's fifth stage, when an adolescent usually pursues the formation of identity, is critical in the development of the ability to live well. It subsumes the childhood identity elements of trust, autonomy, initiative, and industry and forms the necessary basis for the next stage, intimacy. Since Erikson connects these two stages so closely, they will be treated together in this psychohistorical analysis of Scott and Zelda Fitzgerald.

Adolescence, for both Scott and Zelda, was primarily a social event. Early in their identity struggles they had firmly established their attitudes toward work. Scott was certain he wanted to be a professional writer, while Zelda strongly denied the need for any significant work goal in her life. These solutions, however, to one part of their identity problems did not lessen their growing pains either before or after they met and married, because each brought to their relationship fragile identities based upon the unresolved problems of childhood. Intimacy therefore was always a thorny problem for the Fitzgeralds.

Moreover, as we have seen, neither possessed a fundamental sense of trust. The public effects of these and other past psychological deprivations was an almost hostile non-conformity with accepted social roles and institutions. For a long time the Fitzgeralds' behaviour, though it charmed certain elements of the New York society and press, managed to hide from Scott and Zelda the deeper motives of guilt and self-hatred that made self-destructiveness so attractive.

Erikson has labelled such anti-social conduct the sign of a "negative identity" since it is based upon identifications that society believes are dangerous.[32] In most cases, including those of Scott and Zelda Fitzgerald, this process is the result of a search for some place where an individual can exist without demands made from an over-solicitous society, that is, the demands of parents, peers, government, church and so on. It is a "desperate attempt at regaining some mastery in a situation in which the available positive identity elements cancel each other out".[33] Such a choice may be a lonely flight from the clear obstacles of reality. Often it ends without the attainment of any firm identity, the foundation of an individual's desire for sustained intimacy. This, unfortunately, was the common fate of Scott and Zelda Fitzgerald.

From Scott Fitzgerald's earliest days as a member of the fashionable St. Paul, Minnesota community until his death in Hollywood, he always used his talents to promote his own social success. Yet any satisfaction was usually short-lived. He would let praise and notoriety go to his head; his charm soon became a strident egotism that very few people would tolerate for long. This recurring pattern in Fitzgerald's social behaviour seemed almost automatic until late in life when perhaps it was too late. Still, such destructive behaviour should come as no surprise considering the negative experiences of his early years. Their cumulative effect made it almost impossible for Fitzgerald to benefit from the major crises of those first three stages of Erikson's life cycle which are the foundations of a secure identity. Mistrustful of his own instincts and filled with deep feelings of guilt and inadequacy, the only course open to the adolescent Fitzgerald was once again to conceal these weaknesses behind various forms of overcompensation. This meant the construction of an unreal outer-directed identity that relied almost completely upon social approval while neglecting the supreme value of a strong inner core. Nor did this choice put Fitzgerald out of step with his peer group because adolescents "are sometimes morbidly, often curiously, preoccupied with what they appear to be in the eyes of others as compared with what they feel they are, and with the question of how to connect the roles and skills cultivated earlier with the ideal prototypes of the day".[34]

According to the self-appraisal Fitzgerald made when he was fifteen, he possessed a *"sense of infinite possibilities"*. This energizing trait was one of the main reasons Fitzgerald became a "fierce perfectionist" as he confronted the struggles of adulthood. He seemed to demand from himself and his relationships what he felt was lacking in his primary childhood identifications with adults, especially his mother and father, whose inadequacies were more deeply etched upon Fitzgerald's mind than Grandfather "P. F." McQuillan's romantic success. For Scott this nineteenth-century Horatio Alger always symbolized his and America's dream of fame as well as the chivalrous desire to win back the lost glory of his family name.

A vital factor in the reshaping of Fitzgerald's poor childhood identifications with the older generation and a redeeming element in his identity development appeared when Fitzgerald was sixteen and a student at Newman. There he met Father Sigourney Webster Fay, a trustee of the school who would soon become the headmaster. Immediately there sprang up between them a close rapport that parallels in many ways Fitzgerald's description in *This Side of Paradise* of the warm, father-son relationship that exists between Father Darcy and Amory Blaine. Considering Fitzgerald's psychological deprivation and Fay's attractive personality, it is easy to understand their friendship. For, according to Arthur Mizener, Fay was

> a man of taste and cultivation who, having never known anything but the life of the well-to-do, had that unconscious ease and security in it which Fitzgerald always envied and never could achieve. In addition to these qualities he was something of an eighteen-nineties aesthete, a dandy, always heavily perfumed, and a lover of epigrams. To a schoolboy of both social and literary ambitions this combination of characteristics must have been nearly irresistible. As a convert to Catholicism Fay could sympathize with Fitzgerald's dislike of the dreary side of his Irish Catholic youth and also show him a Catholicism which was wealthy and cultivated and yet secure in its faith.[35]

For eight years, until his death in 1919, Father Fay was an unusually pervasive influence upon the adolescent Fitzgerald. The
degree of Scott's admiration for him can be seen in the affection-
ate portrait of Fay as Father Darcy and the dedication of his first
novel to him. There is little doubt that Fay satisfied Fitzgerald's
need for a strong and romantic father figure. More than this, he
was a major part of that time in Fitzgerald's life when an adolescent ardently searches for men and ideas to believe in, and whose
service would also offer opportunities to prove oneself trustworthy. At this time the adolescent is eager to be confirmed by
teachers and inspired by worthwhile "ways of life". Since Fitzgerald's concept of Catholicism had always been so negative, his
need to identify closely with a religious figure like Fay during his
adolescence is most significant in evaluating the place of guilt
in Fitzgerald's struggle for identity.

When Fay died suddenly of pneumonia in 1919, Fitzgerald wrote
Shane Leslie that "my little world made to order has been shattered by the death of one man".[36] Although this was a sincere
statement of Fitzgerald's feelings about Fay, we must not lose
sight of the fact that he often disregarded Fay's prudent advice,
though such behaviour is natural for a struggling adolescent. Fitzgerald's relationship with Fay helped to change his view of himself, the world, and his father. This elegant clergyman became a
healthy ideal Fitzgerald incorporated into his own personal life.
No doubt he drew upon his memories of Fay while composing the
idealized portraits of Nick Carraway's father in *The Great Gatsby*
and Dick Diver's minister father in *Tender is the Night*. As usual,
Scott found it easier to overcome his conflicts in his art than in
his daily battles with himself and other people, especially women.

Unfortunately, no female equivalent of Father Fay came into
Fitzgerald's life during adolescence to help change the poor
image of women his neurotic mother had thrust upon him. The
women Fitzgerald sought out at Princeton and afterwards were
beautiful, rich, and socially unavailable. They usually had many
of the qualities his mother lacked. Although his attraction often
transformed him into a passive partner, Fitzgerald's relationships
with these women were both intense and painfully short-lived. This
is often the result when an insecure male like Fitzgerald seeks a
sense of identity through involvement with a socially-prized beauty.
Erikson warns that such "friendships and affairs become desper-

ate attempts at delineating the fuzzy outlines of identity by mutual narcissistic mirroring: to fall in love then often means to fall into one's mirror image, hurting oneself and damaging the mirror".[37]

In January 1915, when Fitzgerald was a socially successful student at Princeton, he met a special mirror, Ginevra King. She was a celebrated beauty, a member of Chicago's monied aristocracy, but also a refreshing nonconformist. Fitzgerald immediately fell in love with her. She possessed so much of what he wanted to see in himself, but his urgent, idealizing quest for identity through a quick intimacy eventually destroyed the relationship. Their fairy-tale romance was mostly a product of the U.S. Mail. As Ginevra later said, they only spent about fifteen hours together. When Scott was not with her he was riddled with a jealousy rooted in his lack of self-confidence and his fear of her rich and highly placed suitors. Yet the most damaging element in their relationship was that Fitzgerald, typically, "over-dreamed" the whole affair, often confusing fantasy with reality, an effect of his own vision of himself as a weak man incapable of winning her. This affair had a lasting effect upon Fitzgerald. Ginevra was the beautiful princess for whom he, the devout knight, sought fame and honours at Princeton. She was the first woman who had given substance to an ideal his imagination would never forsake.

When Fitzgerald gave up the chase in January 1916, he was left with the memory of "a love affair that was still bleeding as fresh as the skin wound on a haemophile".[38] The stories he wrote at Princeton are mostly about Ginevra. This was Fitzgerald's way of struggling to understand the reasons why their love had died. No doubt his longing for Ginevra partially motivated his dogged pursuit of Zelda Sayre and served as the model for his portrait of Gatsby's timeless love for Daisy Fay. To the end of Fitzgerald's life the thought of Ginevra could bring tears to his eyes. Twenty years after they had parted, he saw her again in Hollywood, and almost fell in love once again with this overimagined figure from his past. Fitzgerald the ironist also saw the positive side of his affair with Ginevra. While at Princeton he wrote "The Pierian Spring and The Last Straw", a story in which the hero-writer regains his lost love but in the process destroys his desire to write. More substantially, Ginevra's loss helped to solidify Fitzgerald's drive to be a great writer, literary successes becoming a temporary substitute for the "golden girl".

46

In June 1918, when Fitzgerald was an officer stationed at Montgomery, Alabama, he received the news that Ginevra King was to be married in September. A few weeks later he met Zelda Sayre. According to his Ledger he "fell in love on the 7th" of September with this popular girl of eighteen who possessed "marvelous golden hair and that air of innocent assurance attractive Southern girls have".[39] Many in Montgomery commented that they looked enough alike to be brother and sister. Their similarities, however, extended beyond appearances into the deeper level of common psychological experiences and development where their mutual attraction may be better understood.

When Scott and Zelda met, both were entering a "psychosocial moratorium"—a time when a young adult tries to work out a firm philosophy of life and further strengthen his identity. To many they seemed an enchanted predestined couple, but outsiders could not see the fearful insecurities that had for so long motivated the development and responses of this handsome officer from Princeton. Nor could they possibly believe that Zelda's uninhibited life style stemmed from anything but a firm belief in her own superiority and beauty. Apparently only she knew how much she needed her protective façade and how long it had taken to build it; even Scott was slow to recognize the similarity in their identity problems and defences.

Like her future husband, Zelda had been obsessed with her external image for a long time. In fact this image was all the identity she felt she possessed or could count on. As a student attending Sidney Lanier High School, she cared very little how slovenly she looked during the day. Life for Zelda did not exist in the classroom, but at ballet recitals and "script" dances where her feelings of inferiority gave rise to various forms of provocative antics. Moreover, Zelda knew when to use a particular trait or ploy to her best advantage. She was attractive, even striking, but not beautiful; so her familiar tendency to overcompensate pushed her to wear rouge and mascara before any of the other girls her age had attempted to use such daring cosmetics. Deep down Zelda felt she needed this added glamour; this truly made her a beautiful person with a unique identity, whose stunning appearance and popularity would ultimately remove the pains of insecurity.

For the normal teenager the developmental stages before the identity stage can afford a certain amount of functional strength even if these earlier crises were not sufficiently resolved. Zelda's condition, as we have seen, was different. None of the previous four crises was resolved well at all. What alternative did an adolescent have who had no true sense of trust in herself and others; who lacked a sense of autonomy, but was prone to deep feelings of shame and doubt; who lacked a firm basis for initiative, but was burdened with feelings of guilt about her inadequacies; who had no interest in school or the industry needed to form a proper sense of work? Her chances for establishing a firm identity were rather slim. In response to these childhood conditions Zelda chose a "negative identity". She believed society had victimized her. Therefore people, even her family, with their norms and traditions would no longer restrict her behaviour in any way. Not content just to casually ignore the dictates of society, Zelda openly flouted them; the rouge and mascara were only the beginning.

Completely ignoring the warnings of chaperones at the script dances, Zelda danced cheek-to-cheek with her partners. She "boodled" with the young men of Montgomery in their cars; she drank gin or corn liquor cut with coke, smoked cigarettes when it was still taboo for women, swam in the nude. Zelda graphically acted out her negative identity. Respectable girls did not associate with the likes of Zelda. Moreover, they realized they could never compete with her in their pursuit of the young men of Montgomery. This fact and her aura of confident superiority cut Zelda off from maturing relationships with girls. Being isolated from her peer group became Zelda's best defence and most serious enemy.

By choosing a negative identity Zelda was implicitly saying that she was indeed trying in her own way to discover some meaning in her life. Her choice apparently indicated a scorn of the general public of Montgomery, but this impression was not completely true. Zelda did care, no matter how well she rationalized or blocked out her feelings about people or how often she reminded herself that these same people who were absent or who had never helped her in the past had no right to judge her behaviour now. Her rebellious insistence on placing Zelda first was primarily motivated by self-protection, not selfishness. "It is easier for the patient to derive a sense of identity out of a total identification with that which he is least supposed to be than to struggle for a feeling of reality in acceptable roles which are unattainable with his inner means."[40]

Zelda's negative identity reinforced her original mistrust of herself and of others, especially those of the opposite sex. This was clear from her inability to maintain a mutual relationship with one particular young man during her adolescence and especially during her "engagement" to Scott. Historically the choices for a sexual role available to a young Southern belle were limited. The words of a toast by a member of the Key-Ice Club at the University of Alabama are typical. "To woman, lovely woman of the Southland, as pure and chaste as this sparkling water, as cold as this gleaming ice, we lift this cup, and we pledge our hearts and lives to the protection of her virtue and chastity."[41] Though this image of the submissive yet calculating Southern belle may have been repugnant to Zelda, still this was her world. Even if she firmly challenged its rules, she still felt the emotional effects of the conflict which, in her own words, made it " 'very difficult to be two simple people at once, one who wants to have a law to itself and the other who wants to keep all the nice old things and be loved and safe and protected' ".[42]

Zelda's anxiety about her role as a woman was further complicated by her mother. Minnie Sayre was always a poor model as a woman and mother. Once again circumstances forced Zelda to form her own idea of what a woman, and later a wife, should be. The least painful solution to this problem for the adolescent Zelda, a solution that would also lessen any threats to a poor self-image, was to continue playing the role of the fearless tease, who constantly put her many admirers to the test. In this way she established a sexual role based upon the undesirable identifications her society had condemned for decades. Burdened with this distorted view of her own feminine role she had great difficulty understanding the role of the opposite sex, as may be seen in the accounts of her courtship and marriage to Scott. He, like Zelda, had failed to resolve his childhood crises, leaving him insecure and a victim of overcompensation. Yet Zelda could not tolerate weaknesses like her own or allow herself to recognize their painfulness. Since neither could recognize the destructive power of these mutual similarities, their life together was far from a romantic idyll. The tormenting struggle of the Fitzgeralds to relate to each other is the title to the story of their marriage, a unique, deeply flawed love affair between two individuals with malformed identities attracted to each other precisely because of this similarity.

49

From the moment the Fitzgeralds met at a Montgomery country club dance in July 1918, it was instant romance. Edmund Wilson noted, "if ever there was a pair whose fantasies matched . . . it was Zelda Sayre and Scott Fitzgerald".[43] For the first time Scott felt that he "had found a girl whose uninhibited love of life rivaled his own and whose daring, originality, and repartee would never bore him".[44] And she felt deeply about him in return. Later in her life Zelda remembered that first night when they danced. "There seemed to be some heavenly support beneath his shoulder blades that lifted his feet from the ground in ecstatic suspension, as if he secretly enjoyed the ability to fly but was walking as a compromise to convention."[45]

Fantasy was not all the Fitzgeralds shared. Scott was helplessly drawn to Zelda's magical social world where she seemed to control so effortlessly by her dominating vitality the admiration and acclaim of so many young men. To enter such a competitive sphere and ultimately possess Zelda as his wife Scott believed would certainly enrich his fragile self-confidence. Nor would he not fail to compare her to his lost love, the dark, seductive, and rich Ginevra King. Although Zelda was the exact opposite in appearance, Scott saw her as surpassing Ginevra's beauty in her air of confidence and superiority stemming from a firm recognition of her own attractiveness. After their marriage he wrote Edmund Wilson that Zelda's most important influence on him was her "complete, fine and full-hearted selfishness and chill-mindedness".[46]

Fitzgerald, like many others, was easily seduced by Zelda's façade. She in turn quickly realized how different Scott was from her previous beaux. He possessed intelligence, discipline, wit, social standing—the attributes she lacked and wanted. Still, she sensed a basic kinship of spirit between them. Both shared the same dream of an exciting, adventurous life in New York. Zelda believed she could not enter this world of glamour and loneliness without someone like Scott to shape her life. Unknown to her he felt the same way. He needed Zelda for her vitality that gave meaning to his life. For adolescent love is "to a considerable extent . . . an attempt to arrive at a definition of one's identity by projecting one's diffused self-image on another and by seeing it thus reflected and gradually clarified".[47] Doubtless, Zelda, like Scott, had fallen in love with a projection of herself. Intimacy, however, had to threaten such an illusory love since, lacking a firmly delineated sense of self, she must inevitably have experienced love as "an interpersonal fusion amounting to a loss of identity". Therefore while allowing Scott to come closer, she continued her familiar pattern of diverse, noncommittal relationships with other men. They provided Zelda with the continual attention she had never received from the first man in her life, her father, a craving that seemed forever unsatisfied. Moreover, since Scott was infatuated with her, she knew competition from other men provoked his desire for her further. Yet for all her feminine tricks Zelda would become jealous and angry whenever Scott dated another girl. In short Zelda loved and wanted to possess him, but she also wanted to keep intact her private vision of herself as a liberated belle that no man could claim as his alone.

As the summer of 1918 drew to a close, Scott tried to press Zelda for some kind of commitment. Psychologically she was not ready for such pressure. Then too, whether Scott would be shipped to Europe was uncertain. This was the main reason he pressed her for a decision, and one of the reasons why Zelda was wary of binding herself. Another governing factor in her hesitation was Judge Sayre's disapproval of Scott's excessive drinking. Zelda subconsciously really wanted to please her father. By delaying the decision she believed she was being the dutiful daughter. Fortunately for Zelda, Scott was sent in October to Camp Mills, Long Island, to embark for Europe. While he was preparing to go overseas the Armistice was signed. Scott returned to Montgomery to await his discharge and, more importantly, continue his pursuit of the elusive Zelda.

When the Fitzgeralds reunited at Montgomery a sexual relationship developed which Scott later described as "sexual recklessness". It troubled his Irish Catholic conscience but caused Zelda little or no guilt. She even continued to date other men and recounted her activities to Scott. This careless game that played with Scott's deepest feelings was just another sign of Zelda's inability to accept fully her role and emotions as a woman and to put herself in his position. On a deeper level this immature sexual relationship can be seen as self-seeking and based in a search for identity; each partner is really trying only to reach himself. Zelda never intended to be maliciously cruel. Her fault was a lack of self-understanding. In fact they were both like children indulging in a form of "masochistic one-upmanship". When Zelda dated another man, Scott in retaliation turned to drink. An argument and reconciliation took place. She would see another man again; he would start drinking again, and so on. Nevertheless a strong part of Zelda still wanted to spend her future with her fairy prince, First Lieutenant Fitzgerald, in the enchanted city of New York. Scott, in turn, seemed hypnotized by this wildly popular Southern belle whose appeal overwhelmed his imagination.

Afraid of another failure, Scott accepted Zelda on her terms and went off to New York to build the life they had both dreamed about. Zelda remained in Montgomery still seeking out the best young men. Once again she kept Scott well informed about her romantic escapades, and for him this period was lived in "a haze of anxiety and unhappiness". He could not understand Zelda, her shifting moods or her activities. Had he been able to analyse his own motivation, then, perhaps, his reactions to Zelda would have been different. Her behaviour clearly indicated that she lacked that "firm self-delineation" which is the prior condition of true intimacy, although such a deficiency does not rule out less fulfilling forms of love. She needed and sought out her identity through a relationship with a weaker, controllable man. Zelda articulated this attitude in a letter to Scott. "People seldom interest me, except in their relation to things, and I like men to be just incidents in books so that I can imagine their characters."[48] It seems that Scott could not see that Zelda's defence against people was in thinking of them as inanimate objects with no feelings. In this way they could not hurt her and she was safe.

As their separation stretched into months, Zelda became more impatient with Scott's lack of success in New York. Her letters became less frequent. More significantly she became pinned to a young golfer and upon second thought "accidentally" returned the fraternity pin with a sentimental note to Scott. Curiously this tactic did not anger him. Instead it reduced him to begging Zelda for a quick marriage. She responded by breaking the engagement, an action Scott basically admired because he believed the girl really worth possessing would not wait long for anyone. The next five months they remained apart.

Zelda continued her hectic dating and gloried in her scandalous reputation. Scott, after a drunken binge that lasted several weeks, turned very systematically to rewriting his novel, *This Side of*

Paradise. On 16 September 1919, he received a special delivery from Scribner's that they wanted to publish his work. A few weeks later Scott went to Montgomery and Zelda accepted his marriage proposal. On 26 March 1920, *This Side of Paradise* was published. For Fitzgerald its immediate success was only overshadowed by his marriage to Zelda Sayre on 3 April 1920, in the rectory of Saint Patrick's Cathedral. It was a joyous time for Scott. He had achieved his primary goal, Zelda, but, more importantly, not by imitating her flamboyant behaviour. His novel basically had been the product of disciplined, hard work. In addition the money he made from the sales of *This Side of Paradise* meant something very special to Fitzgerald. "It made it possible", as Elizabeth Janeway points out, "for him to have Zelda; just as important, it validated his confidence in himself and in his talent to the point where he felt he was a match for her."[49]

Zelda's initial response to Scott's good fortune reinforced his growing sense of achievement. Shortly before their marriage she claimed that "it was her mission in life to help him realize his potential as a writer".[50] Scott took her almost literally at her word. The result was a creative and destructive confusion of art and life which essentially manifested throughout their harrowing relationship the desperate need the Fitzgeralds had for one another. He assumed that Zelda's life, her manner of thinking, experiences, words, letters and diaries, and finally, her "illness", were his exclusive literary property. Zelda, therefore, became both Scott's wife and favourite character, the "raw material" for a succession of fictional heroines—Rosalind, Gloria, Daisy, and Nicole—that merged with Fitzgerald's own experiences to supply the subject matter of his completed novels and several of his short stories.

Scott, however, was well aware of Zelda's essential relationship to his identity as a man and a writer who depended upon transparently autobiographical "material". Almost paralysed by his love of her vital personality, Fitzgerald, one feels, viewed the two of them as one person. Nor, as he openly confessed, could he depict how anyone thinks except himself and possibly Zelda.

Zelda, at first, believed she wanted this kind of dependent intimacy. Unaccustomed to the sophisticated life of New York and drawn to the protective fame and urbane ways of her husband, she readily welcomed a life where there was little need for her to struggle for a separate identity or role. Zelda, however, soon became increasingly restless. Sensing a slow loss of control in her relationship with Scott, she grew resentful both of her role as the wife of a celebrity and the time her husband spent writing. Her previously hidden feelings of inadequacy came to the surface, intensified by her minor position in New York Society which, unlike Montgomery, left her craving for attention more unsatisfied. "What shall the carefree, vital Zelda do?" then became one of the most distressing problems the newlywed couple had to face. At this point in the marriage Zelda clearly lacked the desire for any specific idea of work, either for personal ambition or money. Moreover, other problems appeared that were equally serious and generally traceable to Scott and Zelda's deeply-rooted psychological problems.

During their courtship the Fitzgeralds would not look at the storm warnings about their relationship. This blindness continued during the early months of their marriage. Life was frenetic and disorganized; almost every night centred around a party where speak-easy gin flowed freely. Still this pace did not black out all their simmering hostilities about each other. Scott's friends remembered very well their bitter public arguments about Zelda's indifference to her duties as a housewife. Her laziness and indifference no longer seemed so attractive to Scott. He now saw them as symptoms of deeper psychological problems. Nor was Zelda without grievances about her husband. Success had not changed the basic Scott Fitzgerald. Behind his façade of intelligence and wit there still lived a fearful, insecure man. His failure to dominate all other men, even bouncers at cheap clubs, meant that Scott's manhood and love for her were essentially weak. There were other trivial matters in their life which triggered their mutual insecurities. She was particular about her food, Scott was not; he had to sleep in a hermetically sealed room, she wanted to have at least one window open; he wanted to change clothes twice a day, Zelda simply let the dirty laundry pile up in a closet while her husband fumed about a lack of fresh clothes.[61] Though these are minor differences that every newly married couple must face and work out, Zelda and Scott were still much afraid of allowing their relationship to deepen in any way. Zelda especially realized how dangerously close Scott was coming to her true self which she felt he obviously did not like. To avoid any further intimacy they both resorted to a form of "distantiation", an attempt to repudiate or

destroy someone with whom one also tries to be intimate. In between parties the Fitzgeralds did this very effectively by a pattern
of argument based upon "overvaluation of small differences" followed by loving reunions. Even the birth of their first child
Scottie, on 26 October 1921, did little to change their style of
relating to one another. For Zelda, in particular, the egocentric
baby of her own family, motherhood offered little or no fulfilment. When she found herself pregnant again a few months after
Scottie's birth, the Fitzgeralds agreed they did not want another
child so soon. Zelda underwent an abortion that apparently left her
emotionally unscarred but stirred up in Scott deep feelings of guilt
and anger at the "chill-mindedness" of his wife.

Such adolescent behaviour was dangerous for their marriage as
well as harmful to Scott as a writer. In March 1922, his second
novel was published, *The Beautiful and Damned*, the story of Anthony and Gloria Patch and their decaying marriage. The reviews
were generally disappointing. Many of the critics speculated about
the author's private life. With this in mind Burton Rascoe of the
New York Tribune persuaded Zelda to review her husband's new
book. On the surface the review was self-conscious and lightly
humorous. Yet her emphasis upon the parallels between Gloria and
herself indicated her identification with the unflatteringly portrayed heroine in the novel. Most likely Zelda's future desire to
write was the product of the success of this review. Why this should
be is easy enough to see: writing for Zelda became a way of rebelling against Scott's control over her since their marriage. Secretly
she wanted to compete against him and at the same time defend
herself against her husband's fictional characterizations of women,
both be herself and what he required of her.

Near the end of 1923 the Fitzgeralds decided to seek out some
peace by a change of location. Scott wanted to work on another
novel which was to be *The Great Gatsby*, and Europe seemed to be
the logical place. Soon Scott was writing again. This took up most
of his time. Servants took care of Scottie and other household
chores. Under such conditions there was little for Zelda to do but
bask in the sun and fantasize, until a young French aviator,
Edouard Jozan, appeared on the scene. Zelda was immediately
attracted to the masculinity of his lean, bronzed body under the
starched uniforms. Beyond this, "There was an air of assurance
about him, a quality of natural leadership that Zelda respected

55

and responded to. Leadership, athletic prowess, a smart military air were precisely those qualities Scott Fitzgerald lacked. It was as if Jozan and Fitzgerald were opposite sides of a coin, each admiring the other's abilities, gifts, and talents, but the difference in the equipment they brought to bear on life was clear."[52]

At first Scott viewed Zelda's relationship with Jozan as purely platonic. He was used to young men falling in love with his wife. A few weeks later he realized how far matters had gone. For Zelda, who was slowly realizing how unfulfilling her relationship with Scott was, Jozan was another barrier to any growing intimacy between Scott and herself. He could also be used to destroy the relationship completely if she so wished. For Scott the affair broke their tenuous bond of trust. He felt deeply betrayed. On 13 July he delivered an ultimatum to them which he later referred to as the "Big Crisis". Although Zelda told Scott she was in love with Jozan and wanted a divorce, her dependence upon him had grown so strong that she quickly abandoned both the relationship and her plans to leave Scott.

The whole experience left a lasting rupture in the Fitzgerald marriage. Thereafter their already weakened relationship steadily deteriorated. Scott neither understood nor tried to understand what had drawn his wife toward Jozan. He refused to see that behind Zelda's deep unhappiness and feelings of uselessness there remained an adolescent girl precisely because only a firm sense of inner identity marks the end of the adolescent process and allows movement "beyond identity" into true intimacy. When a person loses all outer signs of importance, as Zelda had during this time in Europe, oftentimes she is forced in desperation to "redelineate" herself. What she yearns for is a person who will unify the fragments of her self. Such a man was Jozan. But the relationship was short-lived because such a delineation shifts abruptly out of a person's fear of being absorbed into another's identity. Frequently these shifts manifest themselves by an impulsive flight into sexual promiscuity, excessive drinking or work, and even attempted suicide.

Shortly after Jozan left, Zelda took an overdose of sleeping pills. Still Scott could not admit that their relationship would never be the same or that Zelda was a very troubled woman. Their sexual relations became less and less frequent. Scott, however, went back to his work on *The Great Gatsby*; apparently the crisis did not affect his ability to write. In a letter to Perkins Fitzgerald described this time of marital discord as "a fair summer. I've been unhappy but my work hasn't suffered from it. I am grown at last."[53] He was unhappy because he could not tolerate the casual affairs which were common in the Twenties, especially when he had given himself completely to his feelings about Zelda. Mizener writes about Fitzgerald that "Sexual matters were always deadly serious to him, a final commitment to the elaborate structure of personal sentiment he built around anyone he loved, above all around Zelda. His attitude was the attitude of Gatsby toward Daisy, who was for him, after he had taken her, as Zelda was for Fitzgerald, a kind of incarnation."[54] The damage done to this structure of emotions by Zelda's affair was irreparable. It also had a subtle effect upon Scott's conception of the heroine in his fiction, the fatal female with destructive tendencies. A month after the crisis Fitzgerald wrote in his Ledger, "Zelda and I close together", and a few weeks later, "Trouble clearing away". But years later he confessed in his Notebook "That September 1924 I knew something had happened that could never be repaired."[55]

Zelda, unfortunately, did not have work to return to after the affair. Her life once again was devoted to the monotonous dissipation of sun-bathing and partying at night. In public the Fitzgeralds presented a united front. Like her husband, Zelda was inwardly damaged and unhappy. Although he had his writing, she had no career or "ideology" which would serve as "some durability in change", and a basis for developing some sense of fidelity and identity.

Slowly but relentlessly signs of Zelda's deteriorating mental condition began to appear. Within six months of her failed love affair she developed an extreme case of colitis, a probable effect of the psychological stress Zelda experienced after internalizing her anger at Scott's refusal to acknowledge her desperate unhappiness. This painful illness lingered for an entire year, making her and Scott very anxious about her health. It was at this time that Zelda, desperately trying to find a life for herself, first began to paint (it was to become a life-long pursuit), and Scott met Ernest Hemingway. Nothing could have worsened Zelda's relationship with Scott more than his growing admiration for the young, charmingly tough Hemingway. They were spending a great deal of time together. Soon Hemingway was calling Scott his best friend, while Fitzgerald, disappointed with the poor sales of *The Great Gatsby*, constantly praised the work of the younger Hemingway who, schooled as he was in combat and journalism, seemed more mature to him.

After the Jozan incident "distantiation", the counterpart of intimacy, increasingly motivated the Fitzgeralds' mutual behaviour. Zelda tried very successfully to distract Scott from his writing and his friends, especially Hemingway, whom she termed "bogus". Scott, in turn, was wary of any relationship Zelda tried to build, especially if it involved a man. Her only close companions were Gerald and Sara Murphy, and they could not prevent her sinking deeper and deeper into depression. Seeing Scott sitting adoringly at Isadora Duncan's feet at a French inn, she felt that even for that moment she had lost to another woman her only liaison agent to the tangible world. Partially out of a death wish, partially out of that desperate need for Scott's attention and repossession, Zelda stood up on her chair, leaped past Gerald Murphy and down a steep stone stairwell. She miraculously survived.

The Fitzgeralds remained in Europe until December 1926. Their relationship and behaviour became increasingly unpredictable and destructive. Occasionally the Murphys would try to discipline them, but their influence was short-lived. While this "great time" was going on Fitzgerald conceived the plan for a novel on matricide which was originally entitled *The World's Fair*. Later it was renamed, successively, *The Boy Who Killed His Mother* and *Our Type*. In 1925 he wrote to Perkins that his new work was "about several things, one of which is an intellectual murder on the Leopold-Loeb idea. Incidentally it is about Zelda & me & the hysteria of last May and June in Paris."[56] After many changes and much time *The World's Fair* became *Tender is the Night*.

Back in New York, Zelda found difficulty justifying the advantages of being a flapper in a city "glutted, stupid with cake and circuses". The Jazz Age was hysterically coming to an end. More and more Zelda began to live through her daughter. Scott, however, still managed to break through Zelda's slow withdrawal from daily life and fantasies. He began the year 1927 by accepting a job in Hollywood from United Artists to write an original screenplay for Constance Talmadge. During their two-month stay in the film capitol, which Fitzgerald described as "a tragic city of beautiful girls", Scott became infatuated with a young actress, Lois Moran. Unspoiled, seventeen, blonde and blue-eyed, she was an ideal stimulus for a man obsessed with the fear of growing old. Their relationship was an innocent flirtation with Lois wanting Fitzgerald to be the leading man in her next picture. In fact Scott never saw her except when her mother was present since Zelda, no matter what she ever did or said, was always the only woman in his life. But Zelda did not take this friendship with Lois very lightly. Inwardly she felt she was losing her "man" to this "charmer on the edge of girlhood". Zelda confronted Scott and he denied any guilt. But they often quarrelled about Lois, especially after Scott invited her to visit them when they were settled in the East.

After eight weeks of hard work in Hollywood Scott finished the script which was later rejected. Immediately the Fitzgeralds left on a train for the East. During this trip they once again argued about Lois Moran when Scott told Zelda he had invited the young actress to visit them once they were settled in Wilmington, Delaware. The argument reached its climax in Zelda's most symbolic gesture about their marriage; she threw her diamond and platinum wristwatch out of the window of the train. This was the first gift of value Scott had given her during their courtship in Alabama. Still this act, the implications of which Scott surely understood, did not cause him to stop Lois Moran from visiting them as soon as they moved into their new home.

Maxwell Perkins had suggested the locale of the Fitzgeralds' new home because Scott said he needed a quiet place to finish his novel. But once they moved in, both he and Zelda continued their destructive life style. Soon they were giving what John Dos Passos called "Those delirious parties of theirs; one dreaded going. At Wilmington, for instance, dinner was never served. Oh, a complete mess. I remember going into Wilmington—they lived some miles out, trying to find a sandwich, something to eat. A wild time."[57] Without the vital stimulus of his favourite character, Zelda, Scott could do little writing. Both of them drank and smoked and quarrelled too much. Yet when the mother of a close friend, Margaret Winthrop Chanler, asked Scott what was his ambition, he answered, " 'To stay married and in love with Zelda and write the greatest novel in the world.' "[58] Guilt-ridden by his failure to pursue these goals seriously, Scott reproached his wife for not working at something professionally. Instead of rebelling at such hypocritic taunts, Zelda spitefully decided to succeed when her husband was failing. She wrote four articles, three of which were published in 1928 and attributed to both Fitzgeralds. Scott's insecurity and worry about "material" was so obsessive that he would not allow her even this small sign of independent success. Zelda next turned to dance with one purpose in mind, to become as she said, "a Pavlova, nothing less".

Gradually, by the kind of discipline and hard work Scott once possessed, Zelda built a new world of her own through her dancing. She worked at it with a feverish intensity that bordered on the grotesque because she needed immediate success. Dance for her became a form of identity, a release from idleness and emptiness, something very personal that would break her almost complete subjugation to her husband. She describes in *Save Me The Waltz* the fulfilment she sought from her work. "It seemed to Alabama that, reaching her goal, she would drive the devils that had driven her—that, in proving herself, she would achieve that peace which she imagined went only in surety of one's self—that she would be able, through the medium of dance, to command her emotions, to summon love or pity or happiness at will, having provided a channel through which they might flow. She drove herself mercilessly. . . ."[59] Since Zelda had taken dancing lessons as a child and had been highly praised in Montgomery, dancing also was an attempt to return to the safe and carefree world of her childhood. This regression became so compelling that when she was not dancing or practising she was busy playing with and catering to Scottie. One of Zelda's projects was to design a dollhouse for her daughter. This simple structure soon became an elegant palace covered with her paintings and illustrations of animals and scenes from fairy tales, a very clear sign of her movement into a child-orientated schizophrenic world.

Dance, however, became Zelda's main obsession and not the healthy whim Scott originally thought it was. Still he could not see beyond his own problems. Mired as he was in his novel and distracted by the loss of morale that came from writing potboiler short stories for the *Saturday Evening Post*, writing became a painful chore that only drinking could alleviate. His friends, especially Perkins, were concerned by what they kindly called "Scott's nerves".

Fed up with Wilmington the Fitzgeralds went back to Europe where Gerald Murphy introduced Zelda to Madame Lubov Egorova, the head of the ballet school for the Diaghilev Troupe. Under her direction Zelda practised eight or more hours a day. "What had begun as a defiant response to Scott's praise of Lois Moran's ambition and energy had become Zelda's sole preoccupation."[60] Scott's condition was deteriorating but now he could not avoid the implication that Zelda's new style of life was an obvious retreat from him and Scottie. When she was not dancing, Zelda kept to herself and brooded in silence. Scott seemed powerless to deal with the new Zelda. This feeling had been building since the Jozan affair when he found that he was no longer able to satisfy Zelda sexually. They had tried unsuccessfully to have another child, hopefully, a boy. Their failure caused Scott to have further doubts about his masculinity. Zelda tried to deal with her own feelings of sexual inferiority by accusing Scott of being a homosexual. The charge had an astonishing effect. For a time he began to believe seriously that he might really be a homosexual. These doubts caused Scott to put an end to their sparse sexual intimacy. With it went a large part of what remained of his fragile identity and marriage.

The Fitzgeralds returned to Wilmington for a short while in 1928. In the spring of the next year, nearly a decade since the beginning of the Jazz Age, they boarded ship for Genoa. At this time Scott, his novel still incomplete, wrote Perkins "I am sneaking away like a thief without leaving the chapters. . . . I haven't been able to do it. I'll do it on the boat and send it from Genoa. A thousand thanks for your patience—just trust me a few months longer, Max—it's been a discouraging time for me too but I will never forget your kindness and the fact that you've never reproached me."[61]

Throughout their third stay in Europe Zelda's mental health and appearance continued to deteriorate. Her world was entirely consumed by an intense creative urge to become an accomplished dancer. She said: "I worked constantly and was terribly superstitious and moody about my work; full of presentiments. . . . I lived in a quiet, ghostly, hypersensitized world of my own. Scott drank."[62] Zelda also began to burst out into laughter for no apparent reason. She looked physically wasted and even her voice changed. Her relationship with Scott violated all rules of human conduct. Their marriage had now completely turned from collaboration to vicious competition. Often it was no more than a bitter contest that paralleled the Divers at their worst. Neither could help the other because each was deeply engaged in a battle for personal survival against a sinister drive towards self-destruction that was rooted in deep psychological similarities. Yet they both clung to each other like prodigal partners because they had invested much emotion in their relationship. All this was clear to their friends whose signs of affection for them became the triggers for their feelings of paranoia and cruelty. Scott was very close to emotional bankruptcy. Sara Murphy wrote Scott at this time: "You don't even know what Zelda and Scottie are like—in spite of your love for them. It seemed to us the other night (Gerald too) that all you thought and felt about them was in terms of *yourself*. . . . I feel obliged in honesty of a friend to write you that the ability to know what another person feels in a given situation will make—or ruin lives."[63]

Zelda, worn and lonely, once again attempted suicide. This time she tried to seize the steering wheel of their car from Scott and drive both over a cliff. Ironically, the final blow for Zelda came as the result of an offer to join the ballet company of the San Carlo Opera in Naples. If she had accepted she would have been the soloist in *Aïda* with promises of other roles during the season. This was Zelda's chance. She turned it down out of guilt and a mixed fear of failure and success, but the decision shattered her precarious world. For the next few months she drifted helpless and isolated in her private unreal world until 23 April 1930. On that date, slightly more than a decade after her marriage, Zelda entered Malmaison Hospital in Paris. The crisis of true intimacy was now over for the Fitzgeralds. Ahead would be the frustrating agony of trying to repair a relationship that would be, as Scott himself described it, "less a romance than a categorical imperative". Although the first stage of their flawed intimacy had ended in disaster, a different kind of mutual attachment developed. Scott finally had to face the issue of Zelda's illness and his share of the blame when Dr. Oscar Forel and other prominent doctors such as Paul Bleuler, a distinguished authority on psychosis, told him that she was a schizophrenic whose chance for full recovery was one in four. Paradoxically, hearing this, Fitzgerald, a man who greatly respected his father's Southern "breeding" and was always attracted to lost causes, became dedicated to Zelda's recovery.

Until the end of his life he felt a deep need to "protect" Zelda, who responded to such care with expressions of dependent love and anger or contempt. Yet on several occasions, seeing the crippling effect her illness had upon Scott's life, Zelda selflessly asked for a separation or a divorce. Although sorely tempted, he refused. Scott could not give her up. Nor could he stop drinking, although Zelda's doctors believed this was the most serious obstacle blocking some form of tolerable life together. So they loyally clung to one another, oftentimes an unbearable pairing amid harrowing situations. But to call the Fitzgeralds' marriage a failure is a myopic view which overlooks the painful, often mysterious complexities of identity and intimacy in each person's always incomplete search for fulfilment. Scott's summation of their relationship acknowledges so beautifully this enigmatic condition of life. "Perhaps 50% of our friends and relatives would tell you in all honest conviction that my drinking drove Zelda insane—the other half would assure you that her insanity drove me to drink. Neither judgment would mean anything. . . . We have never been so desperately in love with each other in our lives. Liquor on my mouth is sweet to her; I cherish her most extravagant hallucinations."[64]

Dr. Forel's pessimistic diagnosis of Zelda's case was as specific a diagnosis as could be arrived at in 1930. Almost fifty years later, however, a more satisfactory analysis of her condition can be set forth. She suffered from Hebephrenia, a chronic form of schizophrenia characterized by frequent occurrence of bizarre acts of infantilism and almost always associated with a poor prognosis. Many of Zelda's symptoms point to this type of schizophrenia which is often difficult to differentiate from that of the paranoid. Grandiose delusions and hallucinations are common. The mood may be depressed; more often it is one of apathy and detachment, interrupted occasionally by apparently humorous and childlike behaviour. The patient often smiles, giggles or uses grotesque gestures in situations that seem completely inappropriate. Language disorders and neglect of personal habits become prominent in the behaviour of the victim of Hebephrenia.[65] Because of the virulence of this form of schizophenria, Zelda spent the last eighteen years of her life in and out of various institutions. The time and length of her lucid moments were always unpredictable. Such a psychological state indicates the hopelessness of Zelda's pursuit of the Eriksonian apex of maturity, generativity. Success at this stage of the life cycle involves a turning of the self toward guidance of the next generation, usually one's own children. Where there are no children this concern may be expanded into "other forms of altruistic concerns and creativity".

Zelda's relationship with Scottie was never very close because she was unable to express openly how much she truly cared for her daughter. Illness robbed Zelda of her daughter's presence and of what little rapport they shared. Moreover, Scott adored his daughter. With Zelda ill, he felt he had to be both a father and mother to Scottie. His care for her was all inclusive, strict yet gentle. It was Fitzgerald, as Turnbull writes:

> who planned the games at Scottie's parties, who worried about her clothes and saw to it that she had the right kind of ballet slippers. He gave her a lot of himself and expected a lot in return. Scottie was under constant pressure to excel—in everything from French to high diving, from tennis to politeness. Fitzgerald wanted her to be both hard and soft, to be able to make her own way, and yet to appreciate the amenities of those who hadn't had to. His idea of hardness did not include dissipation, and his anxiety about moral questions went to ludicrous extremes.[66]

To verify this analysis one has only to read through Fitzgerald's letters to his daughter.

Since Zelda's role as a mother was limited, she chose other forms of creativity as expressions of her generativity, painting and writing. Both started as forms of occupational therapy but soon became both the means whereby she exhibited her creative talents before the world as well as the signs of her growing impulse towards individuality, communication and caring. In the hospital she would usually write and paint two hours of each day. But in 1932 Zelda began to spend more and more of her free time working on a projected novel. Astonishingly, in about six weeks she completed the work, *Save Me the Waltz*, and immediately sent it without Scott's knowledge to Perkins at Scribner's, an action out of character with her strong feelings and proclamations of dependency upon her husband. When Scott finally found out about this and read the manuscript, he was enraged. For the first time Zelda had directly invaded his own domain. Moreover the novel was intensely autobiographical: a major section was an attack on Fitzgerald.

Save Me the Waltz reopened the rift between the Fitzgeralds. Scott had been drinking very heavily and finding it very difficult to continue his novel, *Tender is the Night*. The content of Zelda's book hurt him very deeply. He felt she had used him, his life and material, to her own advantage while he had sacrificed so much of himself and his art to pay her medical bills. He accused her of stealing his novel. Still his main concern was the effect of the book on Zelda's mental state. He did not prevent the book's publication but tried to help. Zelda continued to write and Scott demanded that he pass on everything she wrote before publication. Her writings threatened his sole right to the use of their life as his writing material, but, more importantly, they reinforced certain deep feelings about Zelda and their relationship which he found most painful to evaluate, no less accept, if they were true in some ways. Clearly, Zelda was not nearly his equal as a creative artist. Fitzgerald always considered himself as a professional and his wife an amateur. But in the struggle to achieve authentic role identity, he felt that Zelda had been victorious. A few months before the publication of *Save Me the Waltz* Fitzgerald wrote to Dr. Thomas Rennie, Zelda's psychiatrist: "In the last analysis she is a stronger person than I am. I have creative fire, but I am a weak individual. She knows this and really looks upon me as a woman. All our lives, since the days of our engagement, we have spent hunting for some man Zelda considers strong enough to lean upon. I am not."[67] Even though *Save Me the Waltz* sold very few copies and received only fair reviews, Scott began to loosen the already weak ties between them. He thought of a possible divorce, an idea he later abandoned when Zelda's literary career collapsed with the failure of her first novel. Although she continued to write, painting became a more attractive goal and remained so until her death. Amid the loneliness and pain of mental institutions Zelda discovered within herself a frantic will to live and a creative urge that included a sense of discipline. Unfortunately, very few of those around her understood or valued this limited development of her identity.

At this point in Scott Fitzgerald's life his "forms of altruistic concerns and creativity" were Zelda's health, Scottie's education, and his writing. Without a vital Zelda the last pursuit was his least successful. He had not published a novel for eight years. He tried to blame it on his drinking and on Zelda. Yet in spite of these burdens he managed to make a home and life for the three of them. Fitzgerald still felt his own salvation was inextricably tied to Zelda's. As Arthur Mizener has pointed out: "His conception of what he was trying to do is reflected in Dick Diver's struggle, especially when Dick says: 'Nicole and I have to go on together. In a way that's more important than just wanting to go on.' Over and above his love for Zelda and his desire to save her he had invested too much of his emotional capital in the relation he and Zelda had built together to be anything but an emotional bankrupt if that relation failed."[68] This meant completing his novel, his final statement of his feelings about himself and Zelda, his confession of faith about love, work, beauty and money. So for two years Fitzgerald fought a dogged fight with the demons of insanity and his own liquor. He finally won. *Tender is the Night* was published in April 1934, and received generally tepid critical praise. It was a brief popular success but was soon forgotten. Fitzgerald responded to this public failure by becoming a recluse. His whole personal existence and philosophy had been fed upon the public acceptance of *Tender is the Night*. Now only Scottie seemed a reason to keep struggling, and even this motivation often disappeared.

Few of the Fitzgerald biographers elaborate at length on the emotional breakdown Scott suffered in 1934 and 1935. Although his was not as extreme a case as Zelda, Fitzgerald had for a long time suffered from "psychoneurotic depression". But one night in November 1935, the former laureate of the Jazz Age, white, shaking, and smelling of whisky, packed a briefcase and fled to Hendersonville, a small town in North Carolina. There he checked into a two-dollar-a-day room at the Skylands Hotel and remained virtually isolated for several days. During this time, while eating twenty-cent meals and washing his own clothes, amid smothering memories of his incurably schizophrenic wife, his own failure and deterioration, and his obvious rejection by most of the American reading public, Fitzgerald honestly faced his own "dark night of the soul"—night in which "it is always three o'clock in the morning, day after day",[69] and every small incident, even a forgotten package, has a tragic importance. More than anything Fitzgerald, who looked and felt so much more than thirty-nine, wanted to think out and put on paper as he said, "why I had developed a sad attitude toward sadness, a melancholy attitude toward melancholy and a tragic attitude toward tragedy—*why I had become identified with the objects of my horror or compassion*".[70]

The result of these painful days of self-analysis was Fitzgerald's slow entrance into the last stage of Erikson's life cycle, defined by the polarity of Integrity vs. Despair. The product of this period is wisdom, a felt knowledge resulting from years of experience and insights. It is a wisdom that is manifested by a detached concern with life itself in the face of death. It means an acceptance of the fact that one's life is one's own responsibility. Rather than despair, a man of integrity reworks his life bearing in mind the basic realities of existence: time, death, and the possibility of immortality.

The emergence of Fitzgerald as a man of integrity begins with three essays written while in North Carolina and commonly known under the title "The Crack-Up". These short works, about twenty pages in total length, are fascinating documents written with a casual nakedness, self-mocking humour, and wisdom too deep for tears. Reminiscent of Kierkegaard's *Sickness Unto Death* and Dostoevski's *Notes from the Underground*, they present Fitzgerald's open confession of his loss of identity and emotional bankruptcy. "So there was not an 'I' anymore—," he writes, "not a basis on which I could organize my self-respect—save my limitless capacity for toil that it seemed I possessed no more. It was strange to have no self—to be like a little boy left alone in a big house, who knew that now he could do anything he wanted to do, but found that there was nothing that he wanted to do—."[71]

One year before "The Crack-Up" Fitzgerald had tried to exorcize his private ills in an essay entitled "Sleeping and Waking". Haunted by the effects of his "two cylinder inferiority complex" and crippling Irish-Catholic guilt, he had tortured himself in his attempts to reveal, as he said, "what I might have been and done that is lost, spent, gone, dissipated, unrecapturable. I could have acted thus, refrained from this, been bold where I was timid, cautious where I was rash. I need not have hurt her like that. Nor said this to him. Nor broken myself trying to break what was unbreakable."[72] This written confession basically failed as therapy. But since Fitzgerald was a lapsed Catholic who had broken with the Church literally but not emotionally, confession was a deep need of the soul. So he tried again with "The Crack-Up". This time the effect was more penetrating. For him the writing of these essays became a source of psychological and artistic release, for at the same time that he was purging his demons he was once again exposing and evaluating those archetypal American experiences of which he had written in his novels and of which his own private crisis was a clear reflection. This time however he was not speaking through Jay Gatsby, Dick Diver or his other fictional creations.

After "The Crack-Up" Fitzgerald still had to struggle very doggedly to survive. A damaging story about him in the *New York Post* drove him once again to attempt suicide. Scott was deeply hurt by Hemingway's condescending attitude towards him and stunned by his friend's "public laying of a wreath" on Fitzgerald's career in his short story "The Snows of Kilimanjaro". Then his mother died in September 1936. The tragedy of her joyless life swept over him in a rush. At this time he remarked "Mother and I never had anything in common except a relentless stubborn quality." This quality, his love for Scottie, and a dedication to Zelda kept him alive. Yet Fitzgerald was now a different, wiser man, a man of integrity, as his nurse noted in the fall of 1936. "He wasn't devoid of self-pity, yet he viewed his life with detachment and blamed himself for his plight."[73] Andrew Turnbull describes the wise Fitzgerald as he was about to depart for Hollywood in 1937 where he hoped to fashion a novel from the life of the legendary movie producer, Irving Thalberg.

> Having learned the lessons of success and the deeper ones of failure, he spoke with new authority. Whatever he may have been at the start, he was not the least superficial of men. He had not only grown up, he had grown way beyond the "maturity" most people achieve in a safe, conventional existence, as any reader of his last letters to Scottie cannot fail to notice. Schooled by suffering—some self-inflicted, some not—he had attained a knowledge of himself and of the human condition that may truly be described as tragic.[74]

Less than a week after his arrival in Hollywood Fitzgerald met Sheilah Graham. Their relationship in many ways prolonged his life. Vital and attractive, like Zelda, this ambitious girl from the slums was charmed by the author's tenderness and understanding. In spite of his weaknesses the apex of life for Fitzgerald was caring. Driven by the need to be needed and the need to teach, the mature Fitzgerald took great pleasure in educating his new love in the ways of life and literature. He was not an easy man to live with, especially when out of work at the studios. Oftentimes he quarrelled with Sheilah and separated. Reunion always seemed to follow even the most bitter conflicts. Periodically Scott would go East to take

Zelda on vacations, although he now knew he had to learn to go on without the person who had been so intimate a part of his life and goals. In 1938 he wrote Zelda's doctor, "Certainly the outworn pretense that we can ever come together again is better for being shed".[75]

Fitzgerald had once written "There are no second acts in American lives". But he had gone to Hollywood to prove himself wrong. He was there for much more than money. He wanted to write movies, a new novel, *The Last Tycoon*, which he could not begin until he met Sheilah Graham, and once again recapture the fame of his youth. At first Fitzgerald was successful. Most of the time he was sober and worked almost desperately hard on his writings. But during his second year in Hollywood his hopes turned to disillusionment. In a letter to Perkins he characterized the movie business as "a strange conglomeration of a few excellent overtired men making the pictures, and as dismal a crowd of fakes and hacks at the bottom as you can imagine".[76] Fitzgerald had gained a few screen credits, but as Aaron Latham has pointed out,

> Hollywood had Scott Fitzgerald down as a drunk. He himself had helped to shape that image by writing a story called "Crazy Sunday" which immortalized a party where he had too much to drink and "made a fool of himself in view of an important section of the picture world, upon whose favor depended his career". And there *were* recurrent bouts during Fitzgerald's Hollywood years, from 1937 to his death in 1940, when all his days seemed to be turning into crazy Sundays, when he seemed to be caught up in a drunken party which would not end, when he went on making a fool of himself day after day. Toward the end he couldn't find work.[77]

Although Fitzgerald labelled the Hollywood movie world "nothing more nor less than an industry to manufacture children's wet goods", his failure at screen writing would have broken him except for Sheilah and his work on *The Last Tycoon*. It was to be a tragic novel that "would say something fundamental about America, that fairy tale among nations",[78] and still please two people: Scottie at seventeen and Edmund Wilson at forty-five. Fitzgerald wanted it to be, as he said, "the history of all aspiration—not just the American dream but the human dream and if I came at the end of it that too is a place in the line of pioneers".[79] For him Monroe Stahr became the last product of this race of pioneers. Although

Stahr's fate embodies a critical view of all America, Fitzgerald's unfinished treatment of the producer remains compassionate and wise.

Hollywood had conquered Fitzgerald, yet he would not let this failure stop him from writing *The Last Tycoon*. In October 1939, Fitzgerald began to work full time on the novel. By November he spoke of "digging it out of myself like uranium—one ounce to the cubic ton of rejected ideas".[80] Soon after, he suffered a heart attack. The doctor told him to stay in bed for six weeks. Fitting a desk to his bed he continued writing. On 21 December 1940, while making notes on next year's football team in a "Princeton Alumni Weekly", he had another attack. In a moment he was dead, leaving *The Last Tycoon* forever unfinished, a continual object of conjecture and discussion like the life of its author.

After Scott's death and the publication of *The Last Tycoon*, Zelda began to write her second novel, *Caesar's Things*, "a sort of collage of autobiographical writing, fantasy, and religiosity",[81] which she worked on until her death. She continued her painting; but for Zelda the days were flooded with memories and talk of her life with Scott. She even painted colourful murals from scenes of their life together on the rear wall of her family cottage in Montgomery. Zelda still needed someone or something to care about deeply when the ever-present memories and guilt feelings greatly magnified by her illness became unbearable. Oftentimes she turned to Scottie, her grandson, and mother. Another outlet was a newly-discovered interest in religion that wavered with every lapse into depths of severe schizophrenia. Still it remained a source of strength especially after Scott's death. At the end of 1947 Zelda was forced to leave her mother's home and return to Highland Hospital. She seemed to sense that death was near. Her last words to her mother were " 'Momma, don't worry. I'm not afraid to die' ".[82] On 10 March 1948, Zelda was trapped in a fire on the top floor of the hospital and died there. A week later her body was taken to Maryland where it was buried next to Scott whom she resembled in too many ways.

NOTES

1 *The Letters of F. Scott Fitzgerald*, ed. Andrew Turnbull (New York: Scribner's, 1963), p. 208.

2 Arthur M. Mizener, *The Far Side of Paradise: A Critical Biography of F. Scott Fitzgerald* (Boston: Houghton Mifflin, 1965), p. xvii.
3 Andrew Turnbull, *Scott Fitzgerald* (New York: Scribner's, 1962), p. 4.
4 Erikson, *Identity*, p. 97.
5 F. Scott Fitzgerald, "Author's House", in *Afternoon of an Author: A Selection of Uncollected Stories and Essays*, ed. Arthur M. Mizener (New York: Scribner's, 1957), p. 184.
6 *F. Scott Fitzgerald: A Critical Portrait* (New York: Holt, Rinehart & Winston, 1965), p. 8.
7 "F. Scott Fitzgerald", in *Portraits: Real and Imaginary* (London: Jonathan Cape, 1924), pp. 220–1.
8 Fitzgerald, *Letters*, p. 79.
9 Piper, p. 296.
10 Erikson, *Identity*, p. 106.
11 Piper, p. 4.
12 Mizener, p. 64.
13 F. Scott Fitzgerald. "The Crack-Up", in *The Crack-Up*, ed. Edmund Wilson (New York: New Directions, 1945), p. 69.
14 Nancy Milford, *Zelda: A Biography* (New York: Harper & Row, 1970), p. 6.
15 Milford, p. 9.
16 Milford, p. xii.
17 Milford, p. 8.
18 Milford, p. 147.
19 Mizener, p. 4.
20 Turnbull, pp. 16–17.
21 Erik H. Erikson, *Gandhi's Truth: On the Origins of Militant Nonviolence* (New York: Norton, 1969), p. 125.
22 Turnbull, pp. 34–5.
23 Erikson, *Identity*, p. 117.
24 Turnbull, p. 261.
25 Milford, p. 11.
26 Turnbull, p. 204.
27 Fitzgerald, "Author's House", p. 186.
28 Mizener, p. xxvii.
29 Turnbull, p. 20.
30 Milford, p. 13.
31 Fitzgerald, *Letters*, p. 32.
32 Erikson, *Identity*, p. 174.
33 Erikson, *Identity*, p. 176.
34 Erikson, *Identity*, p. 128.
35 Mizener, p. 44.
36 Fitzgerald, *Letters*, p. 375.
37 Erikson, *Identity*, p. 167.
38 Fitzgerald, *Letters*, p. 578.
39 Mizener, p. 79.
40 Erikson, *Identity*, p. 176.
41 Milford, p. 21.

42 Milford, p. 21.
43 Milford, p. 25.
44 Turnbull, p. 87.
45 Zelda Fitzgerald, *Save Me the Waltz* (Carbondale: Southern Illinois University Press, 1967), p. 35.
46 Fitzgerald, *Letters*, p. 355.
47 Erikson, *Identity*, p. 132.
48 Milford, p. 48.
49 Elizabeth Janeway, *"Zelda: A Biography"*, *Saturday Review*, 13 June 1970, p. 30.
50 Mary Heath, "Marriages: Scott and Zelda, Eleanor and Franklin", *The Massachusetts Review*, 13 (Winter/Spring 1972), 282–3.
51 Milford, p. 72.
52 Milford, p. 109.
53 Fitzgerald, *Letters*, p. 166.
54 Mizener, p. 178.
55 Mizener, p. 178.
56 F. Scott Fitzgerald, *Dear Scott/Dear Max*, ed. John Kuehl and Jackson Bryer (New York: Scribner's, 1971), p. 120.
57 Milford, p. 133.
58 Turnbull, p. 172.
59 Zelda Fitzgerald, *Save Me the Waltz*, p. 124.
60 Milford, p. 141.
61 Fitzgerald, *Letters*, p. 213.
62 Milford, p. 147.
63 Milford, p. 155.
64 Milford, p. 222.
65 Arieti, Silvano, M.D., *Interpretation of Schizophrenia* (New York: Basic Books, 1974), pp. 37–8.
66 Turnbull, p. 223.
67 Milford, pp. 261–2.
68 Mizener, p. 246.
69 Fitzgerald, "The Crack-Up", p. 75.
70 Fitzgerald, "The Crack-Up", p. 80–1.
71 Fitzgerald, "The Crack-Up", p. 79.
72 Fitzgerald, "The Crack-Up", p. 67.
73 Turnbull, p. 281.
74 Turnbull, pp. 308–9.
75 Turnbull, p. 291.
76 Fitzgerald, *Letters*, p. 278.
77 *Crazy Sundays: F. Scott Fitzgerald in Hollywood* (New York: The Viking Press, 1970), p. vii.
78 Turnbull, p. 307.
79 Turnbull, p. 307.
80 Fitzgerald, *Letters*, p. 131.
81 Milford, p. 355.
82 Milford, p. 382.

3
This Side of Paradise:
Amory Blaine

In 1919, the first year of the Jazz Age in America, Scott Fitzgerald substantially revised *The Romantic Egotist* for the third time and retitled it *This Side of Paradise*. The novel was published on 27 March of the following year and became an immediate popular success. The first edition was sold out in twenty-four hours. By July, *Bookman* listed it as one of the nation's best sellers. In less than a year *This Side of Paradise* sold close to fifty thousand copies and was widely referred to as the "bible of flaming youth". Much to the surprise of Fitzgerald he became known almost by accident as the "laureate of the Jazz Age", "a kind of king of our American youth", as Glenway Westcott has put it.[1]

Through the relentlessly analysing voice of Amory Blaine, the youthful romantic hero of *This Side of Paradise*, who triumphantly, although painfully exclaimed at the end of the work, " 'I know myself but that is all' ",[2] Fitzgerald started to tell his own anxious postwar generation that "he felt as they did, that something had to be done with all the nervous energy stored up and unexpended in the War".[3] Moreover, like his contemporaries, he was deeply restless and uncertain of the purpose and scope of life in America. "The war to end all wars" had not really ended in victory and national satisfaction but in disillusionment. The bloody trenches of France where a few yards of dirt cost thousands of young lives were also partially responsible for a widespread questioning of the accepted democratic order and way of life presented to the young by their largely complacent elders.

James E. Miller, Jr., has commented about *This Side of Paradise* that "In spite of the apparently blurred and mixed purposes in the novel, the sexual, social and literary restlessness of the younger generation came through clear enough to capture the imagination of a decade".[4] Without a doubt Fitzgerald's first novel haunted its readers like the beat and lyrics of a popular song.

73

Undergraduates studied it with recognition and compassion. Although full of "bogus ideas and faked literary references",[5] *This Side of Paradise* was a true picture of the American postwar youth. The *New York Times Book Review* claimed that "the glorious spirit of abounding youth glows throughout this fascinating tale. We know that [Amory Blaine] is doing just what hundreds of thousands of other young men are doing in colleges all over the country."[6] Frederick Lewis Allen, an authority on the Jazz Age, has said, in a more expanded form, the same thing:

> A first class revolt against the accepted American order was certainly taking place during those early years of the Post-war Decade but it was one with which Nikolai Lenin had nothing whatever to do. The shock troops of the rebellion were not alien agitators but the sons and daughters of well-to-do American families, who knew little about Bolshevism and cared distinctly less, and their defiance was expressed not in obscure radical publications or in soap-box speeches, but right across the family breakfast table into the horrified ears of conservative fathers and mothers.[7]

In addition to being a commercial success and historically authentic *This Side of Paradise* was a literary landmark, the first popular example to be published in the U.S.A. of the well-established European literary genre, the *bildungsroman*, youth's maturing or coming of age. This form implies that to understand a character fully one must carefully analyse his childhood and adolescence—the often subconscious origins of his development and major external influences on it. Interaction between self and society is at the core of the *bildungsroman* which has asserted that the hero can achieve a sense of identity only through a number of significant confrontations with the world around him.

Few *bildungsromane* continue beyond Erikson's fifth stage. Possessing a firm sense of identity the hero is ready to assume the responsibilities of intimacy and generativity. *This Side of Paradise*, however, leaves the reader with some serious doubts about the solidity of Amory Blaine's identity as a basis for the accomplishments of maturity. After all his various experiences, does he still remain a shallow "philosopher" of the early Jazz Age? Or is he a significant yet unfinished precursor of Fitzgerald's wise and tragic vision of life as it is embodied in the author's more refined and three-dimensional heroes, Jay Gatsby and Dick Diver?

In his first novel Fitzgerald sets forth Amory Blaine's identity crisis. At the end of the work we see an adolescent hero who seeks a union between himself and his imperfect world by transforming society. In the process he hopes to achieve an Eriksonian sense of identity where the *"style of one's individuality"* is confirmed by *"one's meaning for significant others in the immediate community"*.[8] Although his vision is blurred, Amory recognizes similarities between his personal conflicts and the larger upheavals in American society. This recognition supplies him with a new goal in life, the reformation of society into a more acceptable environment. Amory "found something that he wanted, had always wanted and always would want—not to be admired, as he had feared; not to be loved, as he had made himself believe; but to be necessary to people, to be indispensable. . . . Amory felt an immense desire to give people a sense of security" (266). With this choice "The Education of a Personage", the subtitle of the last half of the novel, comes to an end. Amory is no longer an egotist, dominated by self-indulgence and an unexamined dependence on society. He has become a personage who, as Monsignor Darcy explains to him, "is never thought of apart from what he's done" (104). His existence does not depend upon the approval of others. His goals and achievements are rooted in a vision of himself that constantly urges him "to be a certain sort of man"—a man constantly in search of the best forms to "guide and control life".

At the end of the novel Amory Blaine has the same aspiration which Erikson discovered in the early lives of Luther and Gandhi, the subjects of his own two *bildungsromane, Young Man Luther* and *Gandhi's Truth*: the aspiration to transform the world around him to confirm his own personality. Like Luther and Gandhi Amory also wishes to raise his "individual patienthood to the level of a universal one",[9] achieve his identity, and help solve for all what they could not solve for themselves alone. But he still does not possess the means to accomplish such a heavy task. Robert Sklar is right when he says that "Amory Blaine does not 'know himself' in any classic sense. He has arrived at his new form of individualism through a reversal of the Cartesian reasoning, 'I think, therefore I am.' He had knocked away all his props of social place and social convention and found himself still standing. Therefore he could say, 'I am'. But what he was to think had not yet come to him."[10] Amory lacks a new system that will control human

nature starting with himself; he still lacks the vision of a reasonably coherent world which is essential for the vital strength of
hope. He merely tolerates his native Catholic Church as an empty
ritual and "seemingly the only assimilative, traditionary bulwark
against the decay of morals" (281). He considers the possibilities
of socialism; but his bravado arguments, although shocking to his
companions, lack conviction. Even Amory confesses "it's the only
panacea I know" (277). A solution to the problem of an individual's
search for identity similar to that of Luther or Gandhi is not yet
possible for Amory. Even if he evolves a plausible new system for
dispensing justice in life, until Amory resolves those fundamental
crises of early childhood that have condemned him to repeat certain
frustrating patterns of behaviour, nothing will work.

In the short space of five pages at the beginning of *This Side of
Paradise* Fitzgerald directly and expertly does the greater part of
his character exploration of Amory's parents, the key figures of
his childhood. H. L. Mencken, when reviewing the novel, singled
out the whole first chapter for particular praise. "Not since Frank
Norris's day has there been a more adept slapping in of preliminaries."[11]

Fitzgerald's treatment of Amory's parents reflects an important
shift in American parental authority, a shift with debilitating
effects upon offspring. Historically, since the Revolutionary War,
the position of the father as the head of the family and the just
regulator of his offspring's development has been slowly deteriorating until within the past two generations the mother has assumed the place of dominance in the family, in education, and in
cultural life. In America, as nowhere else, the mother stands as a
symbol of the family, the defender of decency and morals. Her
power, a misplaced paternalism, is occasionally of great value in
the training of the children; but more often it is crippling to the
pursuit of identity and maturity.

Reflecting this profound social change, Fitzgerald's portrait of
Amory's father, Stephen Blaine, is sparse. Fundamentally weak,
his influence upon Amory is negligible and in the long run will
cause much more psychological harm than good. Both father and
son are victims of "Momism". Stephen has abdicated his position
of authority and strength within the family in favour of his aggressive wife Beatrice. He has failed to form with her a bond of loving
alliance so necessary for the healthy growth and education of their

son. Instead, after his daily work Stephen retreats to the library where, undisturbed, he can read about the romantic adventures of Byron or peruse the countless columns of facts from an encyclopaedia.

Stephen Blaine's life is far from the "living romance" of Fitzgerald's grandfather, Philip McQuillan. In fact, his only two substantial gains in life, the acquiring of wealth and the winning of his wife, are not the products of courageous and sustained effort but the results of the convenient deaths of two elder brothers and the weary boredom of an international prima donna. His marriage to Beatrice, which she contracted "almost entirely because she was a little bit weary, a little bit sad" (4), is little more than a social façade. Fitzgerald presents their union as basically sterile, one with little growth and intimacy. Each parent neurotically lives his or her own separate life filled with human or material distractions, blind to the fact that the person who will suffer most from their life styles is their precocious only son.

Since Stephen Blaine is weak, passive, and often absent, Amory turns, as a child, towards his mother for a model to imitate. Almost completely unawares he takes upon himself many of her key feminine traits which become the basis of his character. The frequent use of the term "the fundamental Amory" indicates quite forceably that no matter how hard Amory tries to dismiss or conceal the fact, his feelings and words constantly remind him that he is psychologically Beatrice's son much more than Stephen's. Moreover, Amory, as he grows up, realizes the need to break this bond if he is to achieve a firm identity and survive in a world not controlled by a strong mother figure. Indeed, we often cannot understand Amory's thoughts and behaviour until we analyse those of his strangely attractive, yet pitifully comic, mother who is both an aimless alcoholic and a physical and spiritual hypochondriac. An aristocratic Victorian superficially educated in Europe near Lake Geneva, Beatrice is shallow, snobbish and extremely self-centred, except for her smothering love for her son. She is a chronic poseur and a compulsive storyteller about herself and her "companion", Amory. But beneath this tangled network of externals Beatrice is essentially insecure, mistrustful, and lacks a firm sense of identity. She does not know who she is and, what is more damaging to herself and her son, she takes extreme delight in her constantly shifting emotions and behaviour, in the belief that this posing makes her more attractive to her friends, whom she quickly tires of, or to new acquaintances.

Although Beatrice says very little directly to her son about his own spiritual growth, she consistently coddles him and reminds him of the precious value of his physical health. " 'Dear, don't *think* of getting out of bed yet. I've always suspected that early rising in early life makes one nervous. Clothilde is having your breakfast brought up' " (5). And " 'This son of mine,' he heard her tell a room full of awestruck, admiring women one day, 'is entirely sophisticated and quite charming—but delicate—we're all delicate; *here*, you know.' Her hand was radiantly outlined against her beautiful bosom; . . ." (5). When Amory has the scarlet fever, fourteen specialists are called in. When his appendix bursts at sea, "after a series of frantic telegrams to Europe and America, to the amazement of the passengers the great ship slowly wheeled around and returned to New York to deposit Amory at the pier" (7–8).

This "magnificent" overprotection puts Amory into a psychologically ambiguous situation. He feels proud and happy to be the centre of attention, motherly care and love, even if they are extreme and the products of an unhappy marriage. But his mother's scrupulous preoccupation with his well-being also engenders in Amory a strong sense of mistrust about himself, his activities and potential. The constant domination of his mother makes him feel a deep sense of inner and outer fear and fragility. But with a passive and frequently absent father, to whom can he turn for security and strength except his neurotic, self-centred mother?

Along with her obviously excessive preoccupation with Amory's health Beatrice spoils him completely. There are no ordered ways or attempts on the part of the Blaines to guide their growing boy by means of prohibitions and permissions. When Amory does anything wrong Beatrice is superficially horrified but casually dismisses any idea of discipline. Thus Amory, though insecure because of his mother's overcontrol, is introduced very young in life to expectations of almost complete freedom with no limits. If he can garner the strength, a world, which he basically distrusts, is outside waiting to be conquered because he believes other people will treat him as his mother does.

But the growth of personal autonomy depends upon a firmly developed early trust which informs him that he is a separate being with unique needs and the ability to contend with them. Lacking this primary sense of the division between himself and others, Amory finds it difficult to will anything for himself or believes the will of others to be his own. He often wills what others, like his mother, will him to be. Such a fundamental lack of self-possession breeds a strong inclination to feelings of doubt and shame. During Amory's adolescence these negative counterparts of autonomy appear as major parts of his self-image continually causing him severe doubts about his capacity for independence.

As a child, one of Amory's most effective defences against the increase of such feelings of shame and doubt is the development of a precocious conscience that does not allow him to get away with anything. Later in life this "Puritan conscience", as Amory labels it, instead of being a source of comfort causes him great anguish and travail. During adolescence it is a distinct disadvantage. But Amory does not immediately trace this loss of self-esteem to his mother's overcontrol and his later, almost slavish, incorporation of the standards of others as the best guides to personal success and happiness.

Nothing is more characteristic of an individual like Amory who has lost this early battle of autonomy than a lack of both authentic initiative and industry, the psychosocial achievements of Erikson's third and fourth stages, for the sense of initiative actualized at this Oedipal stage of a child's development is the basis of a sense of industry when he begins school. There he "applies to concrete pursuits and approved goals—the drives which have made him dream and play. He now learns to win recognition by producing things".[12] Amory's lack of initiative and failure to develop a sense of industry as an adolescent are consistent with Fitzgerald's portrayal of him as trapped in a still unresolvable Oedipal relationship with his mother.

Since Amory is a victim of the intense affections of a neurotic mother and the unattractiveness of a passive father, as a child he is not able to shift his basic identification from female to male. Thus he has to bear with all the effects of a defective formation of character, especially with a guilt which evolves into an acute state of narcissism. Fitzgerald entitles a chapter of *This Side of Paradise*, "Narcissus Off Duty?" According to the neo-Freudian, Karen Horney, narcissism involves "vanity, conceit, craving for prestige and admiration, a desire to be loved in connection with an incapacity to love others, withdrawal from others, normal self-esteem, ideals, creative desires, anxious concern about health, appearance, intellectual faculties".[13] This ambivalent state of mind afflicts Amory's adolescence, which, unfortunately, starts with his belated introduction to formal education at thirteen when Beatrice suffers a nervous breakdown "that bore a suspicious resemblance to delirium tremens" and destines Amory to spend two years in Minnesota with his aunt and uncle apart from his mother. Until that time private tutors have directed his education as mother and son tour the United States. Amory's four years at schools in Minnesota and Connecticut (St. Regis), "though in turn painful and triumphant", are governed by this failure to resolve his Oedipal conflict. He constantly reproduces his pattern of relating with his mother in his dealings with teachers and peers. Unlike the coddling responses of his mother Amory encounters a hostility and rejection that make the development of a sense of work almost impossible. Soon "he was resentful against all those in authority over him, and this, combined with a lazy indifference toward his work, exasperated every master in school. He grew discouraged and imagined himself a pariah; took to sulking in corners and reading after lights" (27).

At Princeton, to which Amory is attracted by "its atmosphere of bright colors and its alluring reputation as the pleasantest country club in America" (36), he rarely thinks about the importance of the material and techniques offered by his professors. His constant preoccupations are the best and quickest ways toward fame, popularity, and power—football, clubs, "the Princetonian", the Triangle Club.

When Amory does think of the primary aim of the university, the proper communication of knowledge, learning, and technology, he feels guilty because of his laziness and lack of effort but he still satirizes Princeton's antiquated pedagogical methods and looks upon his teachers as gargoyles. He does relatively little work and finally fails mathematics which leads to his dismissal from the university. Once again Amory shows no vital sense of initiative and competence that would help him work through a difficult situation threatening the achievement of those collegiate goals that once meant much to him. Driven by feelings of narcissism and inferiority he continues his pattern of revolt which is really another of Amory's forms of self-punishment. Even Eric, one of the less perceptive characters in *This Side of Paradise*, recognizes Amory's habit of sabotaging his pursuit of an identity. Yet neither Eric nor Amory sees the figure of Beatrice behind this and other self-destructive acts. Even when she is miles away or dead, her education of Amory remains essentially intact, dictating the substance and style of her son's thoughts about himself and others, especially about women and the basic institutions of society.

The more clearly sexual side of this unresolved Oedipal conflict in Amory can be seen in an earlier chapter entitled "A Kiss for Amory". After Amory has been in Minneapolis for two months he receives an invitation to a sleighing party from one of the wealthiest and most beautiful thirteen-year-old girls in the city, Myra St. Claire. Arriving at a late hour, "a lateness which he fancied his mother would have favored. He waited on the doorstep with his eyes nonchalantly half-closed, and planned his entrance with precision" (9). Amory's well-prepared poses and words never materialize because the sleighing party has already left for the local country club, leaving an irritated Myra and an unrefined chauffeur to transport Amory with them in a limousine. In the back seat of the car he romances Myra into avoiding the reproachful eyes of the other guests by slipping into the Minnehaha Club in order to be found later in "blasé seclusion" before the fire. Amory must regain his failed pose which, because of the narcissism he nurtures, requires the continual admiration of his peers. Myra, since she thinks Amory is the "quintessence of romance", seems an easy prey for Amory, who believes a kiss is a sign of masculine superiority. What follows is one of the more notable and evocative passages in *This Side of Paradise*, in which the young Fitzgerald carefully sets down, through Amory, his honest vision of the youth he thought representative of his daring generation:

> Myra's eyes became dreamy. What a story this would make to tell Marylyn! Here on the couch with this *wonderful*-looking boy —the little fire—the sense that they were alone in the great building—
>
> Myra capitulated. The atmosphere was too appropriate.
>
> "I like you the first twenty-five," she confessed, her voice trembling, "and Froggy Parker twenty-sixth."
>
> Froggy had fallen twenty-five places in one hour. As yet he had not even noticed it.
>
> But Amory, being on the spot, leaned over quickly and kissed

81

Myra's cheek. He had never kissed a girl before, and he tasted his lips curiously, as if he had munched some new fruit. Then their lips brushed like young wild flowers in the wind.

"We're awful," rejoiced Myra gently. She slipped her hand into his, her head drooped against his shoulder. Sudden revulsion seized Amory, disgust, loathing for the whole incident. He desired frantically to be away, never to see Myra again, never to kiss anyone; he became conscious of his face and hers, of their clinging hands, and he wanted to creep out of his body and hide somewhere safe out of sight, up in the corner of his mind.

"Kiss me again." Her voice came out of a great void.

"I don't want to," he heard himself saying. There was another pause.

"I don't want to!" he repeated passionately.

Myra sprang up, her cheeks pink with bruised vanity, the great bow on the back of her head trembling sympathetically.

"I hate you!" she cried. "Don't you ever dare to speak to me again!"

"What?" stammered Amory.

"I'll tell mama you kissed me! I will too! I will too! I'll tell mama, and she won't let me play with you!"

Amory rose and stared at her helplessly, as though she were a new animal of whose presence on the earth he had not heretofore been aware.

The door opened suddenly, and Myra's mother appeared on the threshold, fumbling with her lorgnette.

"Well," she began, adjusting it benignantly, "the man at the desk told me you two children were up here—How do you do, Amory."

Amory watched Myra and waited for the crash—but none came. The pout faded, the high pink subsided, and Myra's voice was placid as a summer lake when she answered her mother.

"Oh, we started so late, mama, that I thought we might as well—"

He heard from below the shrieks of laughter, and smelled the vapid odor of hot chocolate and tea-cakes as he silently followed mother and daughter downstairs. The sound of the graphophone mingled with the voices of many girls humming the air, and a faint glow was born and spread over him.

Casey-Jones—mounted to the cab-un
Casey-Jones—'th his orders in his hand.
Casey-Jones—mounted to the cab-un
Took his farewell journey to the prom-ised land. (14–15)

From a thematic and technical point of view this is one of the most suggestive scenes in the novel. Fitzgerald, using the skill at realistic dialogue and sensuous imagery he learned while writing the lyrics and book for the Princeton Triangle Club musicals, launches his hero into his first sexually significant scene. In post-World War II America so delicate a subject as the dawning of sexual desire was certainly not the subject of popular novels. If any dimension of sexuality was dealt with in the fiction of Fitzgerald's day, it was done quickly or was smothered in severe moralism or maudlin sentiment. In Owen Johnson's *Stover at Yale*, a well-known novel about undergraduate life in America that Fitzgerald admired, the hero cannot even hold the hand of a girl, no less kiss and want to kiss more. To the older generation of the Jazz Age, a kiss meant the beginning of a serious commitment between young adults and was surely not the sign of masculine victory in a battle of infatuation fought by young teenagers.

No doubt Myra's and Amory's actions and words in this scene are representative of their generation. But Fitzgerald's unique perception lies in his portrayal of Amory's sexual disgust after one kiss. It is a striking picture of Amory's basic and continual failure to trust women, especially when any form of sex is involved or even implied. The psychoanalytic source of Amory's sexual disgust after kissing Myra is an Oedipal failure. His abnormal closeness and identification with his mother compels Amory to treat every female he gets close to as his mother. He also expects every woman to dominate him as his mother did and therefore he relates to her as an inferior and courts rejection. Feelings of attraction and revulsion seize Amory when he kisses Myra because the image of his mother in Myra draws him on emotionally, while the actual physical contact produces disgust because the stronger feelings of inferiority and incipient incest also rush into his consciousness. To combat these negative feelings Amory, as a child, had turned to narcissism, the construction of an aggrandized self based upon constant praise and admiration. After kissing Myra and being flooded with negative feelings, Amory, imitating his original retreat to narcissism, "wanted to creep out of his body and hide somewhere safe out of sight, up in the corner of his mind" (14). But he fails because his narcissism depends upon external praise and Myra, after he has refused her, turns upon Amory and threatens him. Her reaction renders him helpless. His mother had given him nothing but love, and Amory expects this from all women. The angry, unloving Myra becomes for Amory "a new animal of whose presence on earth he had not heretofore been aware" (15). And when she fails to tell her mother about her experience, this throws Amory into more confusion confirming his lack of trust in himself and women. Beatrice had always made her private life, even her romances, public to all who would listen.

Throughout *This Side of Paradise* Amory's sexual relationships with almost all women except Clara end in defeat or rejection (Isabelle and Rosalind) or in encounters with evil or death (Axia, Eleanor, and Jill). When we leave Amory at the end of the novel, on the road to Princeton, we know for certain that in his mind beauty, sex, evil, and death are all interconnected and surrounded by a negative aura.

> The problem of evil had solidified for Amory into the problem of sex. He was beginning to identify evil with the strong phallic worship in Brooke and the early Wells. Inseparably linked with evil was beauty—beauty, still a constant rising tumult; soft in Eleanor's voice, in an old song at night, rioting deliriously through life like superimposed waterfalls, half rhythm, half darkness. Amory knew that every time he had reached toward it longingly it had leered out at him with the grotesque face of evil. Beauty of great art, beauty of all joy, most of all the beauty of women. (280)

The scene, "A Kiss for Amory", foreshadows this future mental organization. Sex, beauty, and evil are all generally represented by the awkwardly seductive, golden-haired Myra. Evil attached to beauty and incipient sexual longings is suggested not by the apparition of the devil, as in the scene describing the relationship between Amory and Axia, but by the sudden revulsion, disgust, and loathing at the whole incident with Myra that seizes Amory after one kiss. Lastly, the presence of death is brought about in two ways. This first of Amory's many romantic encounters takes place in Club Minnehaha, named after the heroine of "The Song of Hiawatha" by Longfellow. Her fate was to die young because of fever and starvation. Secondly, this scene ends with a folk song about the death of a railroad engineer, Casey-Jones, who "Took his farewell journey to the prom-ised land". "A Kiss for Amory" is not banal. In its own way it is fresh, subtle, and, more importantly, thematically predictive.

"A Kiss for Amory" is indeed suggestive of many of the problems Amory encountered in his lengthy identity crisis; and Myra is more than a beautiful, yet frivolous, teenager. From Amory's point of view she represents issues greater than herself. As Erikson says, "From the middle of the second decade, the capacity to think and the power to imagine reach beyond the persons and personalities in which youth can immerse itself so deeply. Youth loves and hates in people what they 'stand for' and chooses them for a significant encounter involving issues that often, indeed, are bigger than you and I."[14] These words also illuminate Amory Blaine's responses to Monsignor Darcy, to two significant male peers, Dick Humbird and Burne Holiday, whom he meets at Princeton, and to Isabelle Borgé and Clara Page. All these individuals have varying but lasting influences upon Amory during his prolonged identity crisis. In different ways they provide necessary conditions and backgrounds against which he struggles to define his experience and goals.

Fitzgerald's first image of Darcy and his consistently positive characterization throughout the novel make it evident that he is Amory's long sought-after father figure meant to evoke in him mature admiration, trust, and needed identification. The portrait of Monsignor Darcy, patterned after Sigourney Cyril Webster Fay, presents a man of influence, intellect, and contagious charm. He does wonders for the young, groping Amory, opening up for him through his own knowledge and diversified experiences a brilliant, romantic, and sophisticated world. An attractive conversationalist, Darcy speaks with easy facility and wit of Catholicism, politics, philosophy, music, literature, and in particular of his favourite writers, Wilde and Swinburne. During their first half-hour of conversation, Darcy and Amory construct a warm communicative father-son relation. "So they talked, often about themselves, sometimes of philosophy and religion, and life as respectively a game or a mystery. The priest seemed to guess Amory's thoughts before they were clear in his own head, so closely related were their minds in form and groove" (104).

This intimate union, firmly based upon the first positive mutual trust and intimacy Amory had ever deeply experienced, endures, even when they are separated, and grows stronger and more influential after Darcy's unfortunate death. Only then does Amory start to realize fully the formative effect that Darcy has had upon

his restless, young spirit and often aimless actions. This identification helps to fill the fundamental void created so early in his life
by the ineffectual Stephen Blaine. It also initiates the slow, painful
process by which Amory tries to overcome his neurotic psychological dependency upon his mother, an absolute necessity before
he can meaningfully relate to women and achieve his identity.

Darcy stands for security to Amory, "the effect of sunlight"
upon a maturing mind desiring something definite. During the
years of their relationship the Monsignor often helps Amory analyse his temperament and problems. He acts as a discriminating
and prudent corrective for his romantic, idealizing imagination and
his often burdensome inferiority feelings, both of which constantly
confuse illusion and reality. After Amory returns to college he receives several letters from his "spiritual father" which help him to
learn more about himself as he searches for a meaningful code of
life.

Amory clearly chooses Monsignor Darcy because he stands for
what Amory lacks in his life, a sense of rational order in his secu-
lar way of life and a sense of trust in God which Amory's wavering
Catholic faith does not supply. Darcy does not fail Amory. He en-
courages or castigates Amory, gives some serious advice based upon
his experiences but also confesses his dependence upon Amory for
inspiration. Darcy cannot be accused of looking for a protégé. At
best he thinks of himself as a loving but fallible catalytic guide.
He is more interested in Amory finding his own identity. Darcy
sets forth this belief most forcefully when he explains to Amory
the distinction between a socially conforming personality and an
inner-directed personage.

> A personality is what you thought you were, what this Kerry
> and Sloane you tell me of evidently are. Personality is a physical
> matter almost entirely; it lowers the people it acts on—I've seen
> it vanish in a long sickness. But while a personality is active,
> it overrides "the next thing". Now a personage, on the other hand,
> gathers. He is never thought of apart from what he's done. He's
> a bar on which a thousand things have been hung—glittering
> things sometimes, as ours are, but he uses those things with a
> cold mentality back of them. . . . When you feel that your gar-
> nered prestige and talents and all that are hung out, you need
> never bother about anybody; you can cope with them without
> difficulty. . . . You brushed three or four ornaments down, and, in

a fit of pique, knocked off the rest of them. The thing now is to collect some new ones, and the farther you look ahead in the collecting the better. But remember, do the next thing! (104)

Darcy's distinction, the basis for the subtitles of the two books of *This Side of Paradise*, continually illuminates Amory's search for identity. At the prep school, St. Regis, Amory classifies himself as a "slicker", a variation of an egotist or personality, whom he defines as ". . . good looking or *clean*-looking; he had brains, social brains, that is, and he used all means on the broad path of honesty to get ahead, be popular, admired, and never in trouble. He dressed well, was particularly neat in appearance, and derived his name from the fact that his hair was inevitably worn short, soaked in water or tonic, parted in the middle, and slicked back as the current of fashion dictated." During his first two years at Princeton "the best of Amory's intellect was concentrated on matters of popularity, the intricacies of a university social system and American Society as represented by Biltmore Teas and Hot Springs golf links" (26). The two peers who stand for Amory's aspiration to be a "top cat", especially at Princeton, and who also evoke his trust and love, are Dick Humbird and Isabelle Borgé.

Humbird is the ideal aristocratic young gentleman—honourable, courageous, and charming. People imitate his dress and behaviour. His friends that range from the highest class to servants worship him. Without undue effort Humbird is at the centre of affairs. The popularity and prominence that Amory desires but will not work for comes to Humbird almost as a kind of divine gift. Still he is not a complete god, because Amory "felt a curious sinking sensation" when Alec told him "the shocking truth" that Humbird's father "was a grocery clerk who made a fortune in Tacoma real estate and came to New York ten years ago" (78). This fact, however, does not dispel Amory's adoration of Humbird's life style which seems to glorify the false tenet that goals and personal success can be achieved without arduous work and sacrifice. When Kerry tells Amory that he is "a sweaty bourgeois", Amory replies, " 'I won't be—long, . . . But I hate to get anywhere by working for it. I'll show the marks, don't you know' " (46).

For someone of Amory's age, trust in an attractive figure like Humbird and problems with the meaning of work are not unusual. They, as well as other exaggerated feelings and actions, are a part of a state of identity confusion which has existed in Amory for a few years. At Princeton it becomes more acute because college is typically the place where a young man "finds himself exposed to a combination of experiences which demand his simultaneous commitment to physical intimacy (not by any means always overtly sexual), to decisive occupational choice, to energetic competition, and to psychosocial self-definition".[15] The deep anxiety and fear caused by an adolescent's need to know himself and make prudent decisions concerning his adult life style are often accompanied by acute disturbances in the sense of industry (Amory cannot apply himself to studies) and an obsession with time and mortality.

At Princeton the theme of death enters most forcefully into Amory's consciousness with the death of Humbird in a senseless car accident. The suddenness of this incident unnerves Amory, who learns about it from an "old crone" in an old kimono whose voice of "cracked hollowness" leaves a haunting harpy effect. She identifies this once vibrant Princeton aristocrat as the dead corpse stretched out under a roadside arclight, his "face downward in a widening circle of blood".

Humbird's body, a "limp mass", is carried into a shoddy house. Amory follows. Inside he hears a taut yet familiar voice.

> "I don't know what happened," said Ferrenby in a strained voice. "Dick was driving and he wouldn't give up the wheel; we told him he'd been drinking too much—then there was this damn curve— oh, my God! . . ." He threw himself face downward on the floor and broke into dry sobs.
>
> The doctor had arrived, and Amory went over to the couch, where some one handed him a sheet to put over the body. With a sudden hardness, he raised one of the hands and let it fall back inertly. The brow was cold but the face not expressionless. He looked at the shoe-laces—Dick had tied them that morning. *He* had tied them—and now he was this heavy white mass. All that remained of the charm and personality of the Dick Humbird he had known—oh, it was all so horrible and unaristocratic and close to the earth. All tragedy has that strain of the grotesque and squalid—so useless, futile . . . the way animals die. . . . Amory was reminded of a cat that had lain horribly mangled in some alley of his childhood. (86–7)

This is the first of many scenes of pointless violence and death in Fitzgerald's novels and stories, but this one is particularly

evocative and surrealistic. The imagery stresses the cruel irrational-
ity of death that has the power to reduce a man to a "limp
mass".

The first effect of this scene of death is to fracture Amory's
illusion that youth, popularity, and power are indestructible compared to the harsh realities of life. Humbird's death changes
Amory's vision of success, his fundamental goals and hopes for the
future, and even helps cause his scholastic failure. Success through
the Princeton social system and extra-curricular activities no longer
attract him. "Amory plus St. Regis' plus Princeton. That had been
his nearest approach to success through conformity. The fundamental Amory, idle, imaginative, rebellious, had been nearly
snowed under. He had conformed, he had succeeded, but as his
imagination was neither satisfied nor grasped by his own success,
he had listlessly, half-accidentally chucked the whole thing and become again: ... the fundamental Amory" (99).

After Humbird's death Amory becomes more introspective. He
slowly realizes that true success depends upon the development
of a strong identity founded in self-knowledge and constructive
struggle. This activation of latent spiritual potentialities gradually
becomes his principal goal during his last two years at Princeton.
And Fitzgerald almost immediately provides his hero with a new
human model, Burne Holiday, a fellow student who champions the
"questioning aloud" of Princeton institutions such as the revered
club system. Amory soon discovers in him the deeper virtues
Humbird lacked. Burne suggests to Amory a new conception of
moral and intellectual superiority without stolidity or dilettantism.
The power of his integrity radiates "an immediate impression of
bigness and security" (122).

Except for a few disagreements Amory is loyal to his new revolutionary model who courageously asserts his own inner beliefs,
even at the cost of popularity. For Amory, Burne seems to be
scaling intellectual heights where others have failed. "Being Burne
was suddenly so much realler than being clever" (125). Amory
begins to read The Kreutzer Sonata of Tolstoi, searching for the
seeds of Burne's contagious enthusiasm. He starts to spend week-
ends with Monsignor Darcy. Strange, wild-eyed grad students with
eccentric theories of God and government become Amory's frequent dinner guests, to the cynical amazement of his friends at
the Cottage Club. Burne fascinates Amory, perhaps too much, be-

cause his image also becomes an obstacle to his own self-analysis and personal development.

Amory is obviously over-identifying with Burne, a mistake he has already committed with his previous model, Humbird. But this time the losing of himself in the personality of another is not a blind act. Amory constantly looks for Burne's clay feet both in his actions and words. Finally they disagree over the question of good and evil and the war. Amory thinks the war "is the great protest against the superman" (152). Burne's response is to sell all his possessions and leave Princeton in order to "preach peace as a subjective idea" (148). Amory now believes his model has become a fanatic, a cheap pacifist, a pawn in the hands of the enemy. Yet he cannot help but envy Burne's courageous action.

The image of Burne Holiday leaving Princeton in a quietly dramatic manner remains very clear in Amory's mind for a long time. Near the end of *This Side of Paradise*, in the depths of disillusion, Amory still thinks of Burne as a hero, a wise man, on the same level with Monsignor Darcy. But he has "sunk from sight as though he had never lived" (262). For Amory he has become as much a victim of death as Darcy, Jesse, Dick and Kerry. It seems that throughout Amory's identity crisis and life the individuals who best embody his changing goals and aspirations, Burne and Monsignor Darcy, fail or abandon him. Still, within the structure and thematic intentions of *This Side of Paradise* Burne performs a significant task. He furnishes an imaginative, concrete focus for Amory's stirring sense that perhaps true success and identity lie within a person.

Clinton S. Burbans, Jr., has pointed out that Fitzgerald makes the relationships of Amory with Humbird and Burne Holiday parallel to those with Isabelle and Clara, two women who also "stand for" Amory's changing set of values while an undergraduate.[16] Isabelle, like Humbird, embodies Amory's yearning for popularity and power. At the same time their romantic attachment, with its game-playing and childish battles, reveals Isabelle's superficiality and Amory's immaturity and weak sense of identity.

Amory's first meeting with Isabelle is staged by curious, juvenile friends. It is a fine example of two narcissistic youths jousting for romantic dominance; each one tries to probe the other's defensive pose and score with apparently clever and pointed remarks that prove the truth of his or her reputation. Both are truly "Babes in the Woods" as the subtitle of this particular section suggests. Amory and Isabelle make no serious efforts at communication. Their thoughts and words are almost solely preoccupied with his or her own image. Narcissism prevails. Although Amory is aggressive and has a "line", he is still fundamentally a victim of deep inferiority feelings who quickly wants to know precisely from Isabelle how much she thinks of him.

Isabelle's response to Amory's protestations of love is equally egocentric. His wishes are really not very important. Isabelle's chief concern is her own popularity; the identity of the boy is insignificant compared to her image of herself as attractive and the number of men who make her the object of their love:

> What a wonderful song, she thought—everything was wonderful tonight, most of all this romantic scene in the den, with their hands clinging and the inevitable looming charmingly close. The future vista of her life seemed an unending succession of scenes like this: under moonlight and pale starlight, and in the backs of warm limousines, in low, cosey roadsters stopped under sheltering trees—only the boy might change, and this one was *so* nice. He took her hand softly. With a sudden movement he turned it and, holding it to his lips, kissed the palm. (69–70)

The centre of Amory and Isabelle's narcissistic attempts at romance is still the kiss. Circumstances, however, prevent them from sealing a romantic evening with a kiss; and, since they are thereafter separated at different schools, the romance is carried on by mail. Even though Amory finds Isabelle "aggravatingly unsentimental in letters" (80), he writes her rapturous thirty-page documents almost nightly as he attempts to find new words for love. At all costs he tries to shut out the strain of desperate self-seeking that is the basis of their relationship. This recognition would destroy his idealized image of himself and his attempts to construct dreams on surface talk, tender glances, and hand squeezes. Like so many adolescents, Amory idealized women but found it difficult to maintain these exalted feelings when confronted by flesh and blood.

After the tragic death of Humbird, Amory spends a weekend with Isabelle. During this time, filled with a frenzied activity that helps him forget Humbird's accident, Amory finds Isabelle all he had expected. Mistaking classical narcissism for identity and true love

> he looked at himself in the mirror, trying to find in his own face the qualities that made him see more clearly than the great crowd of people, that made him decide firmly, and able to influence and follow his own will. There was little in his life now that he would have changed. . . . Oxford might have been a bigger field.
>
> Silently he admired himself. How conveniently well he looked, and how well a dinner coat became him. He stepped into the hall and then waited at the top of the stairs, for he heard footsteps coming. It was Isabelle, and from the top of her shining hair to her little golden slippers she had never seemed so beautiful.
>
> "Isabelle!" he cried, half involuntarily, and held out his arms. As in the story-books, she ran into them, and on that half-minute, as their lips first touched, rested the high point of vanity, the crest of his young egotism. (89)

The consummation of this romantic kiss signals, not a growing closeness between two young people, but the beginning of the end of their relationship. Almost simultaneously with the kiss Amory's shirt stud rubs against Isabelle's neck and leaves a small mark. This slight happening has the power to fracture their dreamy illusions. After an argument Amory realizes that "he had not an ounce of real affection for Isabelle" (91). But his own image of himself as a conqueror demands that he try to kiss her again and again. When this fails, Amory leaves Isabelle taking sombre satisfaction in the insight "that perhaps all along she had been nothing except what he had read into her" (94). This is an important insight for Amory but not unexpected. Both he and Isabelle are young, basically uncertain, and groping for identity. Under such conditions "friendships and affairs become desperate attempts at delineating the fuzzy outlines of identity by mutual narcissistic mirroring: to fall in love then often means to fall into one's mirror image, hurting oneself and damaging the mirror".[17] Such posturing also often succeeds in hiding from view the threatening sexual aspects of the relationship.

Shortly after his breakup with Isabelle, Amory ironically receives two letters: one informs him of his father's death, the other, from Darcy, concerns Amory's difficulty with sex, a problem that has long bothered him but only comes explicitly to the surface in

Darcy's written words. *"You say that convention is all that really keeps you straight in this 'woman proposition'; but it's more than that, Amory; it's the fear that what you begin you can't stop; you would run amuck, and I know whereof I speak; it's that half-miraculous sixth sense by which you detect evil, it's the half-realized fear of God in your heart"* (106).

When Amory was fifteen there was a suggestion of his awareness of sex. At the end of his list of negative traits he placed "a puzzled, furtive interest in everything concerning sex" (19). After his relationship with the beautiful Isabelle Amory's hidden struggles with sex take the form of a growing sense of sex as an evil force that has the power to overwhelm, perhaps even destroy, him. But this awareness is not the product of the fear of sex and beautiful women; rather it is Amory's fear of the destructive forces in himself which they release. Burbans makes this point clear when he writes, "Amory's sense of evil is thus more than a particular or even generalized guilt; rather, it is his deepening fear that without informing goals and moral restraints, his desires and passions, his feelings and emotions, his imagination and intellect could run out of control in several directions and destroy him and those he influences".[18] To these potentially uncontrollable forces is added Amory's fear of God, the ultimate result of the prevalence of mistrust.

Fitzgerald shows the connection between Amory's sexual situation, his deepening sense of evil, and his need to work through his identity crisis by Amory's three encounters with the devil that take place at various intervals after the end of his romance with Isabelle. As a Princeton undergraduate on a date in New York with a friend, Sloane, and two chorus girls, Amory sees in a café a figure suggesting the devil—a middle-aged man dressed in a brown sack suit who smiles faintly at him. Shortly thereafter the two couples move the party to the girls' apartment for obvious sexual reasons. To further reinforce the atmosphere of evil, the real force in Amory's experience, Fitzgerald fills this scene with images of decay and fire, death and Hell, light, whiteness, and dark. The apartment house is a white-stone building, dotted with dark windows, "flooded with a bright moonlight that gave them a calcium pallor" (112). Inside Axia lays "her yellow head" on Amory's shoulder and "temptation crept over him like a warm wind, and his imagination turned to fire. . . ." (112). Amory decides to give in to his desires. Then he sees the devil again with all his frightening traits sitting on a divan that is "alive like heat waves over asphalt, like wriggling worms. . . ." (114).

> His face was cast in the same yellow wax as in the café, neither the dull, pasty color of a dead man—rather a sort of virile pallor—nor unhealthy, you'd have called it; but like a strong man who'd worked in a mine or done night shifts in a damp climate. . . . Then, suddenly, Amory perceived the feet, and with a rush of blood to the head he realized he was afraid. The feet were all wrong . . . with a sort of wrongness that he felt rather than knew. . . . It was like weakness in a good woman, or blood on satin; one of those terrible incongruities that shake little things in the back of the brain. He wore no shoes, but, instead, a sort of half moccasin pointed, though, like the shoes they wore in the fourteenth century, and with the little ends curling up. They were a darkish brown and his toes seemed to fill them to the end. . . . They were unutterably terrible. . . . (112–13)

Terrified Amory runs out of the apartment and down the long, moonlit street, only to realize that the devil's footsteps are not behind, had never been behind, they were ahead. He was not eluding but following them. This realization shocks Amory and throws him into a blind frenzy as the implications of being under the power of the devil break in upon his insecure mind. He turns into an alley seeking escape from the footsteps and terror and "suddenly sank panting into a corner by a fence, exhausted" (115). Amory screams out for someone stupid, meaning someone good. In answer to his prayer he hears something clang "like a low gong struck at a distance, and before his eyes a face flashed over the two feet, a face pale and distorted with a sort of infinite evil that twisted it like flame in the wind; *but he knew for the half instant that the gong tanged and hummed, that it was the face of Dick Humbird*" (116).

In Amory's mind his former aristocratic hero, whose life had ended in an ugly and futile death, has been condemned to Hell because of his glorified power, popularity, and personal charm. The connections between sex, beauty, evil, death and Amory's fears of what he might become are immediately obvious but not to Amory. His first encounter with the devil is an experience "to which he never succeeded in giving an appropriate value, but which, nevertheless, haunted him for three years afterward" (109).

THIS SIDE OF PARADISE

Shortly after this traumatic experience Burne Holiday entered
Amory's life as a serious force to counter the influence of the
dead Dick Humbird. Almost simultaneously Burne's female counterpart, Clara Page, conveniently assumes a part in Amory's life
through Monsignor Darcy, who sends Amory to visit her. The
woman he meets overwhelms him with her goodness. "She was
immemorial. . . . Amory wasn't good enough for Clara, Clara of
ripply golden hair, but then no man was. Her goodness was above
the prosy morals of the husband-seeker, apart from the dull
literature of female virtue" (138).

Just as Burne Holiday helps Amory to burn away his past goals
of power and popularity and truly begin to define himself, so also
does Clara help him clarify his attitudes toward women by becoming a sanctified Madonna figure for his romantic idealism to
worship. Amory, who finds it so difficult to pray after his encounter
with the devil, goes to church with her. "She was very devout,
always had been, and God knows what heights she attained and
what strength she drew down to herself when she knelt and bent
her golden hair into the stained-glass light" (144). Amory also
"discovers in Clara a woman in whom sex has been translated into
intelligence and vitality"[19] but he does not try to contend with her
in order to dominate, nor does he use her to mirror his own images
of himself. Instead Amory seeks her mature opinion about his
character. He venerates her as someone who can help him clarify
his conception of himself. "Clara's was the only advice he ever
asked without dictating the answer himself—except, perhaps, in
his talks with Monsignor Darcy" (143), and she makes it very clear
to Amory that he must change his behaviour if he is to achieve
an authentic identity. During one critical conversation Clara tells
him:

> "You're a slave, a bound helpless slave to one thing in the world,
> your imagination."
> "You certainly interest me. If this isn't boring you, go on."
> "I notice that when you want to stay over an extra day from
> college you go about it in a sure way. You never decide at first
> while the merits of going or staying are fairly clear in your mind.
> You let your imagination shinny on the side of your desires for
> a few hours, and then you decide. Naturally your imagination,
> after a little freedom, thinks up a million reasons why you should
> stay, so your decision when it comes isn't true. It's biassed."

"Yes," objected Amory, "but isn't it lack of will-power to let my imagination shinny on the wrong side?"

"My dear boy, there's your big mistake. This has nothing to do with will-power; that's a crazy, useless word, anyway; you lack judgment—the judgment to decide at once when you know your imagination will play you false, given half a chance."

'Well, I'll be darned!" exclaimed Amory in surprise, "that's the last thing I expected."

Clara didn't gloat. (143)

Gradually Amory falls in love with Clara, whom he refers to as St. Cecelia. Like his identification with Burne Holiday, Amory matures under her influence, but he also wants to surrender to her what little identity he possesses. He wants to marry Clara but for the wrong reasons. By merging with her Amory seeks salvation from many tortuous struggles; her holiness and goodness will save him from his fear of temptation and evil, especially the kind associated with sex. Since she knows his personality so well, such a marriage for Amory means less pain and struggle in knowing and controlling his life and in developing a unique identity, which he finds so difficult because of his early training. On the subconscious level Clara, as Amory's wife, will bolster his basic feelings of inferiority, originally caused by his mother. Thus, Amory will use her "as a guide in the relearning of the very first steps toward an intimate mutuality and a legitimate repudiation. The late adolescent wants to be an apprentice or disciple, a follower, a sexual servant, or patient to such a person".[20] Clara, however, sees through Amory's pleading of love, labels it as cleverness, and leaves him disconsolate but slightly less conceited. "She was the only girl he ever knew with whom he could understand how another man might be preferred" (146).

With the war and graduation from Princeton Amory reaches the end of the undergraduate portion of his youthful moratorium and identity crisis, but he only partially realizes the significance of his departure from Princeton. Amory believes he is leaving behind his identity crisis while he goes off to fight Germany, which stood for everything repugnant to him, materialism and the vast power of licentiousness. In reality he is still continuing his pursuit of an identity. Only the cast of characters and scenery have changed.

Through the use of an "Interlude" of letters Fitzgerald quickly informs the reader about certain events that will affect Amory's future, the death of Beatrice, the melting away of the family fortune, and Amory's disillusionment with war. Restless and horrified *"of getting fat or falling in love and growing domestic"* (163), Amory returns after the war to America to carry on his quest for an identity. He has changed very little; in Part II of the novel his life follows almost the same general pattern as in the first part. Amory tries to fit into the conventional social moulds of job and marriage, but he is once again disappointed and withdraws into a semi-lethargic search for some basic purpose in life.[21]

A new Isabelle appears, called Rosalind, "a sort of vampire", who childishly treats men terribly yet still possesses an *"endless faith in the inexhaustibility of romance"* (171). Clearly a realist very much addicted to the security and luxuries money can buy, she is fundamentally egocentric and without depth no matter what kind of lyrical phrases Fitzgerald uses to describe and glorify her. Rosalind is just an older, more experienced edition of Isabelle Borgé with the added seductive features of a *femme fatale*. Amory immediately falls victim to her charms. In a short conversation, during which Rosalind ironically refers to herself in monetary terms, a person to be purchased, Amory picks up her imagery. "He: I'd like to have some stock in the corporation. She: Oh, it's not a corporation—it's just 'Rosalind, Unlimited.' Fifty-one shares, name, goodwill, and everything goes at $25,000 a year" (174).

Two weeks after their first meeting, Amory and Rosalind are passionately in love. Amory is even motivated to find a job. He thinks about marriage and a regular existence because "he loved that Rosalind—all Rosalinds—as he had never in the world loved any one else" (189). After five emotion-filled weeks, Rosalind's materialistic self strongly emerges. She breaks her engagement with Amory because he will never be able to support her in the style of life she wishes. "I don't want to think about pots and kitchens and brooms. I want to worry whether my legs will get slick and brown when I swim in the summer" (196). Rosalind even tries to be sentimentally altruistic when she tells Amory "You'd hate me in a narrow atmosphere. I'd make you hate me" (195). But all these excuses cannot hide the fact that money in the form of a millionaire suitor, Dawson Ryder, is more valuable and necessary to her than romance. At the end of "The Debutante" Amory is clearly a foolish and impotent victim before the power of a beautiful woman. He finally leaves, once again defeated and deserted by a woman.

After the affair with Rosalind, Amory undergoes an intense attack of inferiority and identity confusion. Liquor helps for a short period of time. Amory's condition then drives him back to parental figures. He writes to Monsignor Darcy but does not hear from him. He searches for another Clara and finds Mrs. Lawrence, "a very intelligent, very dignified lady, a convert to the church, and a great devotee of Monsignor's" (210). She becomes both a father and mother figure for him. While she reminds him of Darcy, she is also similar to Beatrice "not in temperament, but in her perfect grace and dignity" (211). Her conversations revive his belief in living in the nice place of his mind and he soon finds that "Existence had settled back to an ambitionless normality" (212). But Amory cannot block out every thought about his undeveloped identity, especially in the areas of sexual love and work. " 'How'll I fit in?' he demanded. 'What am I for? To propagate the race? According to the American novels we are led to believe that the "healthy American boy" from nineteen to twenty-five is an entirely sexless animal. As a matter of fact, the healthier he is the less that's true' " (215–16). Amory is still confused about the place and power of sex in his life, although the loss of Rosalind makes him unsocial and condescending towards other women. But his obsession with sex and beauty surfaces again when he is confronted by evil in the form of Eleanor Savage, "the last time that evil crept close to Amory under the mask of beauty" (222).

Eleanor represents everything Amory has feared and consciously rejected: sex, the unfettered romantic will, materialism, uncontrolled passion. Her last name indicates what she stands for; she seems to come out of the stormy late afternoons and the elemental forces of nature. Her attitude towards life is hedonistic. Eleanor claims to have killed her conscience and no longer believes in God. On first sight Amory is extremely attracted to her. "Oh, she was magnificent—pale skin, the color of marble in starlight, slender brows, and eyes that glittered green as emeralds in the blinding glare. She was a witch, of perhaps nineteen, he judged, alert and dreamy and with the tell-tale white line over her upper lip that was a weakness and a delight" (227). Amory calls her Manfred, a character Byron based upon Goethe's *Faust*. Fitzgerald's claim that Eleanor is a witch also fits Byron's character, a student of magic

with certain supernatural powers. Thus as long as Amory and
Eleanor knew each other they "could be 'on a subject' and stop
talking with the definite thought of it in their heads, yet ten
minutes later speak aloud and find that their minds had followed
the same channels and led them each to a parallel idea, an idea
that others would have found absolutely unconnected with the
first" (226). There is mental magic here, but early in their relationship Eleanor had already announced to Amory, " 'I'll be
Psyche, your soul' " (226). Fundamentally, Eleanor represents
Amory's first initiation into sex; he views it as another encounter
with the devil.

This time Amory does not run away. He now thinks of himself as a Byronic Don Juan who has decided to take no responsibility for his life. Filled with emptiness and ennui, he wants only
to drift from one thing to another, make no decisions, no commitments. Amory displays these traits as he embraces "the half-
sensual, half-neurotic quality of the autumn with Eleanor" (233).
Thus Eleanor is the emotional and evil force latent in Amory's
soul, and she leads him for a time in a life of sensuous drifting.

> Often they swam and as Amory floated lazily in the water he
> shut his mind to all thoughts except those of hazy soap-bubble
> lands where the sun splattered through wind-drunk trees. How
> could any one possibly think or worry, or do anything except
> splash and dive and loll there on the edge of time while the
> flower months failed. Let the days move over—sadness and
> memory and pain recurred outside, and here, once more, before
> he went on to meet them he wanted to drift and be young. . . .
> It was all like a banquet where he sat for this half-hour of his
> youth and tried to enjoy brilliant epicurean courses. (232–3)

Finally on a "long farewell trot by the cold moonlight" Amory
and Eleanor put aside the poses they have adopted from Brooke,
Swinburne, and Shelley and reveal themselves to one another in a
discussion of sex. Amory painfully realizes that neither the intellect
nor conversion are any protection against this force. In addition,
Eleanor's blasphemous attack upon the Catholic Church and her
attempt at suicide rip away Amory's thin protective cloak of
materialism to reveal a basically religious spirit. He now sees that
the atheistic romantic will, as Sklar explains, "leads to its nega-
tion, belief in nothing, prostration before crude material power;
and one step beyond lies madness".[22]

When Amory first met Eleanor, his paganism soared. Leaving her after an autumn of drifting and idleness, he perceives very clearly that "this half-sensual, half-neurotic" time has not made him forget his human obligations to himself and the world. On the contrary—and this is the meaning of the chapter's title, "Young Irony"—Amory's sinking into sensuous experiences has made him realize more deeply his strong quest for religious meaning and identity. It also makes his past disillusionments and failures more difficult to face.

In a subconscious attempt to repeat a portion of his happy past while at Princeton, Amory travels to Atlantic City. There, four years before, he had experienced joy, spontaneity, and freedom in the company of four other youths, three of whom have since died. Although Amory is "lulled by the everlasting surge of changing waves", his disillusionment deepens. In despair he longs for death and oblivion.

> He was in an eddy again, a deep, lethargic gulf, without desire to work or write, love or dissipate. For the first time in his life he rather longed for death to roll over his generation, obliterating their petty fevers and struggles and exultations. His youth seemed never so vanished as now in the contrast between the utter loneliness of this visit and that riotous, joyful party of four years before. Things that had been the merest commonplaces of his life then, deep sleep, the sense of beauty around him, all desire, had flown away and the gaps they left were filled only with the great listlessness of his disillusion. (245)

At this point in *This Side of Paradise*, Amory has reached rock bottom. He is the sleepless man racked with guilt and loneliness, the kind of person Fitzgerald would write about in "Sleeping and Waking" fourteen years later. At this time of weakness the devil chooses to confront Amory for the third time in a hotel room which he has occupied as a favour for Rosalind's brother, Alec. During the night the house detective discovers Alec together with Jill, "a gaudy, vermillion-lipped blond" (244). Being caught means he will be liable under the Mann Act. Amory must therefore decide whether he should help the brother of the woman who has rejected his love. Suddenly, "Amory realized that there were other things in the room besides people . . . over and around the figure [Jill] crouched on the bed there hung an aura, gossamer as a moonbeam, tainted as stale, weak wine, yet a horror, diffusively brooding already over the three of them . . . and over by the window among the stirring curtains stood something else, featureless and indistinguishable, yet strangely familiar. . . . Simultaneously two great cases presented themselves side by side to Amory; all that took place in his mind, then, occupied in actual time less than ten seconds" (247).

Amory is caught between two forces. One is evil tempting him not to sacrifice himself and take the blame for Alec's illegal act as it surrounds Jill, an embodiment of sex. The other force, which he later finds out is Monsignor Darcy, advocates self-sacrifice and altruism. Amory's mind tells him that the sacrifice would not be a purchase of freedom but a supercilious act for which Alec would secretly hate him. Then the words of Christ while carrying his cross come into his thoughts *"Weep not for me but for thy children"* (248). Christ's sacrifice also appeared supercilious but it was a pure act of altruism done out of love for all people. From it came resurrection and glory. Without thought of what might happen to himself, Amory decides to perform the sacrifice and help Alec. Almost simultaneously with this, the act of a personage, "Amory felt a sudden surge of joy and then like a face in a motion-picture the aura over the bed faded out; the dynamic shadow by the window, that was as near as he could name it, remained for the fraction of a moment and then the breeze seemed to lift it swiftly out of the room. He clinched his hands in quick ecstatic excitement . . . the ten seconds were up. . . ." (248)

This sacrifice is the first positive move which Amory has made since his affair with Rosalind ended. It also prepares him to realize certain truths about himself at Darcy's funeral. Long ago Darcy, in one of his letters to Amory had explained that *"often through life you will really be at your worst when you seem to think best of yourself"* (105).

Near the end of the novel in the section aptly titled "The Collapse of Several Pillars", Amory learns in a short space of time that Rosalind, still the centre of his painful memories, has officially been engaged to the wealthy Dawson Ryder, his mother's investments have failed meaning the end of his money supply, and of most importance, that Monsignor Darcy has died suddenly. These three losses cause Amory even more anxiety and internal questioning because they intensify the problems of love, sexuality, evil, money, and death, which have preoccupied him for so long. They also form the centre of his thoughts in that crucial last chapter of *This Side of Paradise*, "The Egotist Becomes a Personage".

Standing under the "glass portcullis of a theater in New York", Amory scrutinizes the people passing him on the street with a feeling of detachment. Once again, like his experiences after meeting the devil, he is depressed by the "heavy odor compounded of the tobacco smell of the men and the fetid sensuousness of stale powder on women" (255). But more than anything else he allows his imagination to play upon the numerous unpleasant aspects of city life without money.

> He pictured the rooms where these people lived—where the patterns of the blistered wallpapers were heavy reiterated sunflowers on green and yellow backgrounds, where there were tin bathtubs and gloomy hallways and verdureless, unnameable spaces in back of the buildings; where even love dressed as seduction— a sordid murder around the corner, illicit motherhood in the flat above. And always there was the economical stuffiness of indoor winter, and the long summers, nightmares of perspiration between sticky enveloping walls . . . dirty restaurants where careless, tired people helped themselves to sugar with their own used coffee-spoons, leaving hard brown deposits in the bowl.
>
> It was not so bad where there were only men or else only women; it was when they were vilely herded that it all seemed so rotten. It was some shame that women gave off at having men see them tired and poor—it was some disgust that men had for women who were tired and poor. It was dirtier than any battlefield he had seen, harder to contemplate than any actual hardship moulded of mire and sweat and danger, it was an atmosphere wherein birth and marriage and death were loathsome, secret things. (255-6)

With these words Amory expresses the depth of his alienation and nausea. His vision of the desperate lives of the poor is suggestive of T. S. Eliot's early poetry, *The Waste Land* in particular. For Amory being without money makes him a victim without identity in an acquisitive society where love and sex are loathsome and life pleads for "easeful death". His experience with Rosalind still colours his view of reality. People are rotten because he is alone, without a lover, true friends, and money. The power of the last of these has become an obsession because it has dominated him and taken Rosalind away. Fitzgerald recalls the effects of an experience similar to that of Amory when he writes in "The Crack-Up", "I have never been able to stop wondering where my friends' money came from, nor to stop thinking that at one time a sort of *droit de seigneur* might have been exercised to give one of them my girl."[23]

The deepest motivation, however, for Amory's hatred for the poor is that he is one of them. Jobless and without any other income, he is afraid and disdainful of them because he sees an image of himself forced to live as they do. He believes " 'It's essentially cleaner to be corrupt and rich than it is to be innocent and poor' " (256) for in America there is no identity without money, the commodity that guarantees social recognition and love.

After his vision of the poor of New York Amory boards a Fifth Avenue bus and allows his thoughts to flow out unscreened. Once again they centre around the images of sex, money, death, and evil as they have been represented by significant people during his past life.

> Well, he'd had it—I'll sue the steamboat company, Beatrice said, and my uncle has a quarter interest—did Beatrice go to heaven? . . . probably not—He represented Beatrice's immortality, also love-affairs of numerous dead men who surely had never thought of him . . . if it wasn't appendicitis, influenza maybe. What? One Hundred and Twentieth Street? That must have been One Hundred and Twelfth back there. One O Two instead of One Two Seven. Rosalind not like Beatrice, Eleanor like Beatrice, only wilder and brainier. Apartments along here expensive—probably hundred and fifty a month—maybe two hundred. Uncle had only paid hundred a month for whole great big house in Minneapolis. (259)

Beatrice plays a major role in Amory's stream of consciousness, his father none. He associates her very clearly with sex, money, and death. He has lost Rosalind because he has little or no money, the result of Beatrice's squandering of her fortune on a neurotic self that demanded huge investments in doctors' care, medicine, stained-glass windows and seminary endowments. Her "illnesses" suggest to Amory thoughts of the large religious donations that Beatrice handed over in her sudden bursts of religiosity. Amory could have forgiven his mother anything but this. He speculates whether Beatrice was able to purchase heaven as Dawson Ryder had purchased Rosalind. Amory's negative attitude towards his mother grows stronger as he compares her not to Rosalind, whose short burst of emotional love he cannot forget, but to Eleanor, a Satanic female figure who initiated him into physical sexuality. Both were poseurs and neurotic materialists, both had seduced Amory—his mother smothering him with overprotective love when he was a defenceless child causing a basic mistrust and Eleanor sexually seducing him when he was rather defenceless because of anxiety and disillusionment. But both had changed their basic philosophies about life when facing the spectre of death. After these images, Amory's mind shifts to the apartments he sees from the bus. Money again comes to his mind. But the more significant image is that of the apartment houses he saw the night of the incident with the devil. Beatrice and Eleanor are therefore linked in his consciousness to a sense of evil.

Chastened by loneliness and disillusion "the fundamental Amory" is prepared to begin once again his search for that true self which springs from his unique being. This new attitude is the foundation of identity; and, as Erikson explains, a person experiences the first signs of true identity as something that " 'comes upon you' as a recognition, almost as a surprise rather than as something strenuously 'quested' after".[24] Such is Amory's experience at Darcy's funeral where in "haunting grief" at the death of his friend he carefully looks around at the stricken faces of Darcy's followers. He then realizes what Darcy has meant to them. "People felt safe when he was near" (266). This insight is the chief source of Amory's renewed vitality.

> Of Amory's attempted sacrifice had been born merely the full realization of his disillusion, but of Monsignor's funeral was born the romantic elf who was to enter the labyrinth with him. He found something that he wanted, had always wanted and always would want—not to be admired, as he had feared; not to be loved, as he had made himself believe; but to be necessary to people, to be indispensable; he remembered the sense of security he had found in Burne.
>
> Life opened up in one of its amazing bursts of radiance and Amory suddenly and permanently rejected an old epigram that had been playing listlessly in his mind: "Very few things matter and nothing matters very much."
>
> On the contrary, Amory felt an immense desire to give people a sense of security (266).

At the end of *This Side of Paradise*, during his rambling conversation with Mr. Ferrenby and his chauffeur on the road to Princeton, the degree of change in Amory's basic attitudes and beliefs becomes more clear. He refers to himself as an "intellectual personage" meaning that the real Amory Blaine will persistently struggle with his problems and, above all, rule his future life by reason. He also takes upon himself the burden of what he calls "the spiritually unmarried man", a person also controlled by reason. He "continually seeks for new systems that will control or counteract human nature. His problem is harder. It is not life that's complicated, it's the struggle to guide and control life" (272). In order to give a sense of security to other people Amory must struggle to become these two kinds of persons. No doubt his quest for an identity is still before him. But this time perhaps the results will be different. For Amory "knew he was safe now, free from all hysteria—he could accept what was acceptable, roam, grow, rebel, sleep deep through many nights . . ." (282).

NOTES

1 "The Moral of Scott Fitzgerald", in *The Crack-Up*, ed. Edmund Wilson (New York: New Directions, 1945), p. 323.

2 F. Scott Fitzgerald, *This Side of Paradise* (New York: Scribner's, 1920), p. 282. All further quotations are from this edition; page reference will be indicated after the quotation.

3 F. Scott Fitzgerald, "Echoes of the Jazz Age", in *The Crack-Up*, ed. Edmund Wilson (New York: New Directions, 1945), p. 13.

4 *F. Scott Fitzgerald: His Art and His Technique* (New York: New York University Press, 1964), p. 31.

5 Edmund Wilson, "Fitzgerald Before *The Great Gatsby*", in *F. Scott Fitzgerald: The Man and His Work*, ed. Alfred Kazin (New York: World, 1951), p. 79.

6 Robert Sklar, *F. Scott Fitzgerald: The Last Laocoön* (New York: Oxford University Press, 1967), p. 111.

7 *Only Yesterday* (New York: Bantam, 1959), p. 61.

8 Erikson, *Identity*, p. 50.

9 Erik H. Erikson, *Young Man Luther: A Study in Psychoanalysis and History* (New York: Norton, 1958), p. 67.

10 Sklar, p. 57.

11 H. L. Mencken, "Books More or Less Amusing", *The Smart Set*, 62 (September, 1920), 140.

12 Erikson, *Identity*, p. 124.

13 Karen Horney, *New Ways in Psychoanalysis* in *The Collected Works of Karen Horney* (New York: Norton, 1963), I, 88.
14 Erikson, *Identity*, p. 246.
15 Erikson, *Identity*, p. 166.
16 Clinton S. Burbans, Jr., "Structure and Theme in *This Side of Paradise*", *Journal of English and Germanic Philology*, 68 (1969), 608–10.
17 Erikson, *Identity*, p. 167.
18 Burbans, p. 619.
19 Sy Kahn, "*This Side of Paradise*': The Pageantry of Disillusion", *Midwest Quarterly*, 7 (1966), 184.
20 Erikson, *Identity*, p. 168.
21 Burbans, p. 611.
22 Sklar, p. 54.
23 F. Scott Fitzgerald, "The Crack-Up", p. 77.
24 Erikson, *Identity*, p. 20.

4

The Beautiful and Damned: Anthony Patch

In the introduction to *Identity: Youth and Crisis*, Erikson asks a fundamental yet painfully unanswerable question, "How did man's need for individual identity evolve?" He then tries to answer it: "Before Darwin, the answer was clear: because God created Adam in His own image, as a counterplayer of His Identity, and thus bequeathed to all man the glory and the despair of individuation and faith. I admit to not having come up with any better explanation. The Garden of Eden, of course, has had many utopian transformations since that expulsion from the unity of creation—an expulsion which tied man's identity forever to the manner of his toil and of his co-operation with others, and with technical and communal pride."[1] Since Erikson first used the term "identity crisis" while treating shellshocked soldiers during the Second World War, he has continually anchored man's arduous search for identity in the Christian myth of the Garden of Eden, a traditional chronical of man's primary loss of perfection and innocence. This mythic event sentenced every human being to a life of qualified unhappiness, experienced through the four elemental feelings of loss, conflict, struggle, and imperfect love.

Throughout Fitzgerald's writings there is a poignant sense of this transience and loss, at times an almost overwhelming awareness of dissolution and death. This experience is all the more bitter for his heroes because in their respective ways they are obsessed by intense romantic yearnings, a sense of infinite possibilities, which they believe the limitless material promises of American life will ultimately satisfy. This belief in the goodness of man and nature rejects all the implications of the fall in the Garden of Eden myth. Youth and beauty of the body and spirit are essential requirements of its existence. Inherent in this American belief in unlimited possibility is a failure of a seasoned critical faculty. It is a romantic vision of life that rejects traditional virtues.

Since most Americans have acted out a faith that "heaven" is attained in the devout pursuit of success, money, and romantic love, American artists according to Marius Bewley, have always contended with "the problem of determining the hidden boundary in the American vision of life at which the reality ends and the illusion begins".[2] Although it is tempting, Scott Fitzgerald should not be completely identified with Anthony Patch or any of the heroes of his novels. Unlike them, he understood the element of irrevocable tragic loss that grounded his vision of the American experience. That vision has both psychological and social dimensions. Fitzgerald's heroes possess infinite longings unaffected by the sense of limitation that has governed the values of less rapidly changing societies. Instead they are seduced by a society that engenders extreme romantic desires but fails to offer heroic fulfilments. These men ultimately become disillusioned, fail or even die because there are no worthwhile objects for their love.[3]

The Beautiful and Damned is Fitzgerald's first full-length study of the theme of loss and failure. While generally stressing the meaninglessness of life, it presents Anthony and Gloria as apparently successful at the end. They have broken Comstock's will and received thirty million dollars, but the cost of this wealth has been very high. Both main characters have lost their beauty and youth, Anthony his sanity as well. With such a conclusion Fitzgerald ironically suggests they are failures who are unaware of their damnation. Yet we do not have to wait until the end of this sprawling novel to encounter the sense of loss and failure. It pervades the book which, as William Troy says, "is not so much a study in failure as in the *atmosphere* of failure—that is to say—of a world in which no moral decision can be made because there are no values in terms of which they may be measured".[4]

Anthony Patch's major fault is the inability to distinguish clearly between reality and illusion, the spiritual and the material. He is "a Faustian hero—a man of longing—whose very desires are self-destructive".[5] Feeling "more triumphant than death",[6] the hero of The Beautiful and Damned makes the pursuit of immutable beauty and youth his final goal in life, the fulfilment of which will also achieve for him a satisfying identity society must surely confirm. For Anthony the pursuit and achievement of personal meaning is contingent upon a life of leisure and mobility. Moreover, money and a beautiful young lady, Gloria, who shares his

Romantic idealism, are essential means to the heightened world his unlimited imagination has created—with the help of the strongly reinforcing stimuli of the promises of the American society.

The reality in Anthony's attitude, and those of the other Fitzgerald heroes, as Bewley suggests, is a dimension of the spirit, an intense but poorly understood faith in the possibilities of life; the illusion lies in the limitless enlarging of its material possibilities.[7] Fitzgerald clearly recognized the inadequacy of Anthony's (and Gloria's) view of the world. Although *The Beautiful and Damned* is in some ways thematically unclear, "a novel of unassimilated ideas",[8] as Miller labels it, there is little doubt that its author depicts his hero's yearnings as a Romantic flight from reality doomed to failure. He and his wife search for an impossible ideal world beyond time where natural and moral laws do not exist. Their quest is obsessive, perduring in spite of many obstacles and the realization that time alone gives beauty and youth meaning. The strong influence of John Keats, Fitzgerald's favourite poet, who also felt so deeply the sense of loss and the enhancing effect of death upon beauty, may be seen in Anthony and Gloria's sentiments about their goals in life. Shortly after their marriage Gloria tells Anthony: " 'Beautiful things grow to a certain height and then they fail and fade off, breathing out memories as they decay. And just as any period decays in our minds, the things of that period should decay too, and in that way they're preserved for a while in the few hearts like mine that react to them'. . . . 'There's no beauty without poignancy and there's no poignancy without the feeling that it's going, men, names, books, houses—bound for dust—mortal' " (166–7). Anthony confirms his wife's belief later on when he says, "Intolerably unmoved they all seemed, removed from any romantic imminency of action. Even Gloria's beauty needed wild emotions, needed poignancy, needed death. . . ." (214).

Although Anthony recognizes the ultimate power of time and death, he remains a staunch Romantic irrevocably committed to the attainment of his ideal world of leisure. The force of this aspiration pervades the empty world of *The Beautiful and Damned* and gives significance to its apparently weak and passive hero. It is clear Anthony has an immature grasp of human and social values. He lacks self-knowledge, unaware that Gloria, money, and social success are projections of his uncritical Romantic vision. His final fate is one of substantial deterioration. Our last picture of Anthony is of a disabled millionaire, "a little crazy", his beauty and youth gone. Yet amid all this waste the force of his vision and his commitment to it saves him from the stigma of failure and establishes Anthony's final, albeit crudely tragic, identity. Fitzgerald's characterization of the hero of this novel is a long way from the perfect realization of the mythic Jay Gatsby; still, his story embodies themes that form the essential pattern of the author's mature fiction.

To say that the origin of Anthony's vision is solely the heroic desires American history and society engender in its members would be an incomplete explanation. The ultimate source of his aspirations and identity lies psychologically deeper. The roots of Anthony's character and development are embedded in the primary communication between mother and child. The insufficiencies of this relationship as well as his whole childhood hinder Anthony from forming mature attitudes towards the world and establishing adult intimacies.

Fitzgerald's treatment of Anthony Patch's parents, especially the mother, is sparse and comic, almost ludicrous except for the fact that he surrounds them with the deeply threatening aura of death. This aura suggests their mortality and makes us immediately aware of the primary sense of waste and failure that pervades the novel. Anthony's father, Adam Ulysses Patch, was a "dandy of the nineties, spare and handsome", "an inveterate joiner of clubs, connoisseur of good form, and driver of tandems . . ."(5). He was well-known for his preoccupation with externals and how they would bolster his position in New York society even if this meant he would have very little time to spend with his wife and child. It was more important that he be known as "the first man in America to roll the lapels of his coat" (6). Very little is said about Adam's wife, Henrietta, except that she was the Boston "Society Contralto" who was obsessed with her own voice. She "sang, sang, sang" in public or "to Anthony alone, in Italian or French or in a strange and terrible dialect which she imagined to be the speech of the Southern negro" (6). Henrietta died—"joined another choir", as her husband said, when Anthony was five, leaving him with a weak maternal heritage based upon memories that were both "nebulous and musical" (6).

After his wife's death Adam and his son moved to Tarrytown. He visited his son's nursery for an hour a day but he was almost always under the influence of liquor which made his words "thick-smelling". He promised the growing Anthony to take him on all kinds of trips and excursions, but these promises remained just words except for one trip to Europe when Anthony was eleven. On this trip, Fitzgerald writes, "in the best hotel in Lucerne his father died with much sweating and grunting and crying aloud for air. In a panic of despair and terror Anthony was brought back to America, wedded to a vague melancholy that was to stay beside him through the rest of his life. . . . At eleven he had a horror of death. . . . So to Anthony life was a struggle against death, that waited at every corner" (6–7).

Considering the length of the novel Fitzgerald takes up less space in *The Beautiful and Damned* "slapping in the preliminaries" than he did in *This Side of Paradise*. His aim is more the achievement of an "ironical-pessimistic" tone, the characteristic of a school of fiction Fitzgerald learned about through his friend H. L. Mencken. Yet we can also derive Anthony's failure to resolve his primary crisis of basic trust, the foundation of identity, from his adult manifestations of orality and nostalgia. These modes of behaviour, developed during the first stage of life, predispose Anthony to a characteristically passive manner of interacting with the world, especially with Gloria, his friends, Maury Noble and Dick Caramel, and his enemies, Adam Patch and Joseph Bloeckman.

Erikson divides Freud's oral stage into two successive parts. First the infant accepts what is given and hopefully establishes through a healthy maternal relationship a sense of basic trust, the fundamental source of identity. This is followed by a second incorporative stage characterized by taking in and holding with his mouth, eyes, and ears. Usually the oral stage corresponds with weaning, which "even under more favorable circumstances", "seems to introduce into the psychic life a sense of division and a dim but universal nostalgia for a lost paradise".[9] When a child's experience of mutuality with the mother has been radically impaired, this anxiety is greatly increased and causes notable symptoms.

The Beautiful and Damned offers considerable evidence of these symptoms in Anthony. On the most primitive level they are manifest in his changing attitude toward drink. At Harvard where Anthony "was looked upon as a rather romantic figure, a scholar, a recluse, a tower of erudition. . . . He drank—quietly and in the proper tradition" (8). After returning from Europe to await idly his grandfather's death and money, Anthony "found in himself a growing horror and loneliness" (54). His drinking, now "a proper stimulant", increased a great deal. This habit is obvious to Geraldine Burke, a "faintly intimate" girl friend Anthony dates whenever he feels a need for company.

> "You drink all the time, don't you?" she said suddenly.
> "Why, I suppose so," replied Anthony in some surprise. "Don't you?"
> "Nope. I go on parties sometimes—you know, about once a week, but I only take two or three drinks. . . . I should think you'd ruin your health."
> Anthony was somewhat touched. . . .
> "But you have something to drink every day and you're only twenty-five. Haven't you any ambition? Think what you'll be at forty?"
> "I sincerely trust that I won't live that long." (86–7)

The magic of Anthony's love and marriage to Gloria replaces drinking for a short while. This glow soon passes, apathy sets in, and Anthony finds himself "inclined to quicken only under the stimulus of several high-balls" (192). Heavy drinking becomes the necessary condition for the string of ruinous and self-destructive acts that brings about Anthony's final disintegration.

Adam Patch, Victorianism personified and "a reformer among reformers", disinherits his grandson because he chances upon a drunken party Anthony is giving in his house. Deprived of the millions of dollars he had so long awaited, Anthony spends his days and nights drinking while waiting four and a half years for the court to make a decision about his challenge of the will. The day of the verdict he still begins drinking early in the morning. The smell of whiskey he exudes drives Gloria from the room. Shortly afterwards, Dorothy Raycroft, with whom Anthony had carried on a careless and sordid love affair while stationed in a Southern military camp, suddenly reappears. Her ardent protestations of love on this day that would permanently decide his fate enrage and drive the intoxicated Anthony to violence. He seizes and throws a chair at Dorothy but he suffers the more disabling injury, "a thick, impenetrable darkness came down upon him and blotted out thought, rage, and madness together—with almost a tangible snapping sound the face of the world changed before his eyes. . . ." (446). When Gloria and Dick return from court they find Anthony playing with his childhood stamp collection. Ironically he greets Gloria's news of the reversal of the will, a victory worth thirty million dollars, with the reproach of a borderline psychotic.

Throughout *The Beautiful and Damned* Anthony exhibits other less noticeably oral fixations which are nevertheless related to the unresolved conflicts of the first stage. He takes enormous pride in being an "exquisite dandy" who appreciates the beauty of the spoken and written word. Much of the novel is devoted to long accounts of the hero's pseudo-sophisticated philosophizing and discussions with Gloria, Maury Noble, and Dick Caramel about the meaninglessness of the world. Anthony, after the death of his father, had formed the habit of reading a great deal, often until he was exhausted and fell asleep. Eventually he tells his uncle that perhaps he is "best qualified to write", a declaration that occasions Anthony's sole condescension to work, "a history of the Renaissance popes, written from some novel angle" (15). Oftentimes his conversations, reading, and few attempts at writing are done while smoking cigarettes.

But even more than these various forms of orality, Fitzgerald characterizes Anthony by a sense of psychic division, a form of estrangement expressing a radical impairment of basic trust. The first paragraph of *The Beautiful and Damned* is devoted to a portrait of the hero who at twenty-five, at the height of his bachelorhood, "wonders frequently whether he is not without honor and slightly mad", a thought which alternates with thoughts of himself as "rather an exceptional young man, thoroughly sophisticated, well adjusted to his environment, and somewhat more significant than any one else he knows" (3). The rest of the novel depicts the apparent source and effects of this division and the methods Anthony employs to alleviate the discomfort, chiefly by indulging in "a dim but universal nostalgia for a lost paradise". What he actually longs for is an identity which will heal his divided self. Since Anthony failed to achieve the psychosocial advance proper to early infancy, a sense both of trust and of separateness between himself and the world, his "nostalgia for a lost paradise", usually given up at weaning, is transformed into a yearning for some amorphous ideal he has missed. Anthony's "nostalgia" is for the sense of symbiotic union which antedates everyone's pursuit of an identity. Moreover, his obsession that death, the ultimate loss of self, waits at every corner reinforces the intensity of Anthony's longing. It becomes his conscience, the measure by which he evaluates his adult experiences.

Lacking a sense of his individuality and driven by a doomed "nostalgia for a lost paradise", Anthony's search for identity becomes a series of efforts to unite with some larger identity—money, beauty and youth, marriage—that will make him whole. Throughout this losing process, which Fitzgerald often describes to excess, Anthony's romantic vision is untouched by the values of self-knowledge and authentic intimacy that accept the existence of human limitation. His ideal romantic vision inhibits the growth of the sense of separateness which allows one to relate meaningfully to others and the world. In spite of his education at Harvard and in Europe as well as his extensive reading, the sense of his concrete individuality never penetrated those defences he started to construct firmly as an infant.

But we cannot fully understand Anthony's development by analysing his pathological childhood apart from its connection with society. The mother who is the source of an infant's first experience of mutuality is also a member of a family within a society. She, in turn, must feel a certain healthy relationship between herself and the values of her community based upon a sense of a "reasonably coherent world". For only then can the mother communicate to the child at the level of somatic language that he may trust her, the world, and most importantly, himself.

Anthony's first contact with society is through his mother. Since the evidence of his excessive orality indicates a failure of this maternal relationship, mistrust continued to characterize Anthony's mode of relation to people as he matured. However accurate or derivative it may or may not be, Anthony's perception of American society is that it is fraudulent and meaningless. *The Beautiful and Damned* is filled with negative observations on American politics, culture, education, and sexual mores. Much of this "study in national sociology" (70) was the result of Fitzgerald's falling under the influence of Mencken's pessimistic view of the American democratic system that only a new class of aristocrats could save. Anthony's condescending image of himself as a congressman is more the product of the heavy-handed influence of Mencken's volume of essays *Prejudices: Second Series* (a book Fitzgerald reviewed very favourably) than of his creator's informed imagination:

> . . . he tried to imagine himself in Congress rooting around in the litter of that incredible pigsty with the narrow and porcine brows he saw pictured sometimes in the rotogravure sections of the Sunday newspapers, those glorified proletarians babbling blandly to the nation the ideas of high school seniors. Little men with copybook ambitions who by mediocrity had thought to emerge from mediocrity into the lustreless and unromantic heaven of a government by the people—and the best, the dozen shrewd men at the top, egotistic and cynical, were content to lead this choir of white ties and wire collarbuttons in a discordant and amazing hymn, compounded of a vague confusion between wealth as a reward of virtue and wealth as a proof of vice, and continued cheers for God, the Constitution, and the Rocky Mountains! (56)

Fitzgerald agreed with Mencken's negative assessment of American life; the theme of social revolt is an important theme in the general scheme of *The Beautiful and Damned*. When it first appeared in the *Metropolitan Magazine*, Fitzgerald's work was subtitled *A Searching Novel of the Revolt of American Youth*. But Anthony's rebellious attitude is not as acidly clear as that of Mencken even though, unlike *This Side of Paradise*, *The Beautiful and Damned* contains a major character, Adam Patch, who embodies almost all the worst qualities of twentieth-century American society against which its intensely living youth rebelled. Victorianism personified, he is one of the few individuals who can arouse a deep and sustained response in Anthony. But his response is not completely one of disgust and hatred, though these reactions dominate Fitzgerald's initial portrait of the millionaire.

> . . . after a severe attack of sclerosis, [Adam Patch determined] to consecrate the remainder of his life to the moral regeneration of the world. He became a reformer among reformers. Emulating the magnificent efforts of Anthony Comstock, after whom his grandson was named, he levelled a varied assortment of uppercuts and bodyblows at liquor, literature, vice, art, patent medicines, and Sunday theatres. His mind, under the influence of that insidious mildew which eventually forms on all but the few, gave itself up furiously to every indignation of the age. From an arm-

chair in the office of his Tarrytown estate he directed against the enormous hypothetical enemy, unrighteousness, a campaign which went on through fifteen years, during which he displayed himself as a rabid monomaniac, an unqualified nuisance, and an intolerable bore. (4)

Large sections of *The Beautiful and Damned* are given over to the exposition of Anthony's explicit rejection of the lifestyle Grandfather Patch represents. Yet at the same time Anthony is fatally attracted to what he represents, money, power, success, and most of all, safety. He compares the sense of safety he derives from dealing with his brokers to "the same sense of safety he had in contemplating his grandfather's money" (13), seventy-five million dollars. Although Anthony recoils from the Victorian world of his grandfather, because of his unresolved infantile crises, he is obsessively drawn to the security its money and power offer him. Money becomes for Anthony one of two larger forces in American society, the other being the romance of infinite possibility which draws his divided self into identification with a greater whole and thereby establishes a sense of identity. No matter what he says, Anthony has a deeper attachment to his traditional grandfather than to his own well-articulated beliefs in revolt and the meaninglessness of life. Originally deprived of a sense of trust Anthony, at the deepest level of motivation, still retains a strong need for incorporation, the second part of the oral stage, as his primary manner of relating to the world. His human development has been, and still is, shaped by a need to possess an identity, a feeling of safety, not "in the sense of 'go and get' but in that of receiving and accepting what is given."[10]

This formless passivity, the product of mistrust, dominates almost every area of Anthony's existence. Although he claims he would prefer to live in Europe and he philosophizes endlessly about the emptiness of life, especially American society, Anthony's rebellious self is a façade. Without a sense of trust he has long since lost the "battle for autonomy" and as an adult is almost powerless to will anything strictly for himself. His revolt is a fraud, more pretence than real. It covers the shameful fact that Anthony has a weak will but a strong commitment to his grandfather's fortune. Anthony's life is far from being directionless. He dearly wants, as a sign of success and identity, what American society offers and his grandfather possesses, a huge accumulation of money.

Anthony has incorporated America's standards of success as his basic motivation. Yet he is constantly retarded by a powerful inclination to passivity. Nothing is more characteristic of Anthony than his lack of initiative. He is not a man of action and achievement. Except for occasional lapses he rarely attempts to influence the course of his life. Priding himself upon being a dandy, Anthony questions the whole concept of work: " '. . . I want to know just why it's impossible for an American to be gracefully idle'—his words gathered conviction—'it astonishes me. It—it—I don't understand why people think that every young man ought to go down-town and work ten hours a day for the best twenty years of his life at dull, unimaginative work, certainly not altruistic work' " (65). The essence of Anthony's identity is his capacity to drift "gracefully" amid depression, alcoholism, and the loss of love, beauty, and youth while patiently waiting to be saved. His drifting comes about partially through the illusion of romance. Gloria's beauty and youth for a short while provide Anthony hypnotic respite and identity. His permanent salvation, however, lies in the death of his grandfather, an event that will make him instantly very rich and forever secure. These larger external forces, rather than the difficult process of integrating all his basic conflicts—trust and mistrust, will and shame, initiative and inferiority—with the demands of society, provide Anthony with the engulfing means of his identity and final, although qualified and ironic, success.

Anthony's pursuit of an identity is not an interior journey but an external quest to satisfy, through the limitless possibilities American society offers, his romantic longings for timeless beauty and safety. In various occupational, sexual, and social confrontations the hero of The Beautiful and Damned reveals his fundamental pattern of motivation—an extreme hunger for a lost paradise of symbiotic fusion constantly frustrated by a controlling passivity that will not allow him forcefully to seek satisfaction. This infantile disposition guides Anthony's movement through the various stages of early development and motivates his experiences as an adolescent waiting for an identity whose essence is a passive surrender to an identity larger than himself.

Anthony, who is twenty-five when The Beautiful and Damned begins, remains an arrested adolescent throughout the novel because "only a firm sense of inner identity marks the end of the

adolescent process".[11] Anthony's only sense of adult autonomy
is based upon the merely extrinsic possession of his grandfather's
money. But oftentimes during his prolonged adolescence Anthony
suffers from "identity confusion". He has doubts about the power
of money to satisfy his longings for completion and social success.
During his "psychosocial moratorium" each of Anthony's significant attachments to a man or woman becomes to a considerable
extent, as Erikson says, "an attempt to arrive at a definition of
one's identity by projecting one's diffused self-image on another
and by seeing it thus reflected".[12]

Throughout *The Beautiful and Damned* Anthony is constantly
drawn to communicate with characters like Maury Noble, Dick
Caramel, Bloeckman, and especially Gloria because, as we shall
see, he discovers in them projections of various self-images he has
yet to integrate into one identity.

Anthony considers Maury Noble his best friend. At Harvard
"he had been considered the most unique figure in his class, the
most brilliant, the most original—smart, quiet and among the
saved" (19). This is the only man among all his acquaintances that
Anthony admires and envies. In many ways Maury is another projection of Anthony's self and vision of life. He is more than an
admired friend; he is Anthony's social conscience. Maury, like
Anthony, believes life meaningless. But, unlike Anthony, his perceptions of himself, his friends, and the world are not blinded by
idealistic illusions. This attitude clearly emerges during the mid-
night symposium scene:

> "There's only one lesson to be learned from life, anyway," in-
> terrupted Gloria, not in contradiction but in a sort of melancholy
> agreement.
> "What's that?" demanded Maury sharply.
> "That there's no lesson to be learned from life."
> After a short silence Maury said:
> "Young Gloria, the beautiful and merciless lady, first looked
> at the world with the fundamental sophistication I have struggled
> to attain, that Anthony never will attain, that Dick will never
> fully understand." (255)

Maury's short character analyses of his friends are accurate and precise. Although he is the philosopher of "The Meaninglessness of
Life" within the "general scheme" of *The Beautiful and Damned*,

his cynicism does not render him powerless or passive like Anthony. Maury is not afraid to set up and work for a goal, "to become immensely rich as quickly as possible" (43), even if this means consciously compromising his basic view of life. Such self-knowledge, candour, and action are refreshing in contrast to Anthony's weak pretences. No wonder at their first meeting in the novel Anthony, "nervous as a will-o'-the-wisp, restless—" (20) is quickly at rest in Maury's presence.

⊕In the latter part of 1920, when Fitzgerald was writing the first draft of *The Beautiful and Damned*, he wrote Charles Scribner that the hero was to be "one of those many with the tastes and weaknesses of an artist but with no actual creative inspiration".[13] In Fitzgerald's mind Anthony's romantic longings for timeless beauty and his desire to write fulfil the general requirements of an artist. Yet against Anthony, whom Sklar describes as "the man pathetically torn between creativity and passive cynicism",[14] Fitzgerald places an embodiment of Anthony's artistic desires, Dick Caramel, a functioning creator, a writer.⊕

Certain similarities between Caramel's and Fitzgerald's writing accomplishments are perhaps too obvious. *This Side of Paradise* is mentioned by name. The title of Caramel's first novel, *The Demon Lover*, at one point had been the tentative title of *The Beautiful and Damned*. Dick's descriptions of the joys and burdens of suddenly being a successful writer have the same flavour that pervaded Fitzgerald's statements during the months *This Side of Paradise* was a best seller. Yet Caramel's career, as Fitzgerald presented it in *The Beautiful and Damned*, is not simply a form of thinly disguised autobiography, but, as Mizener explains, it "is half a portrait and half a gloomy prediction—for Fitzgerald exaggerated his faults in this mood—of his creator's future".[15]

Of more importance is Caramel's function as a projection of Anthony's artistic tastes and weaknesses. Caramel denies the meaninglessness of life and believes that he is "contributing" by his talent as a writer. He takes his vocation as a professional writer very seriously, taking notes in public, lecturing his friends on the value of literature, and spending many hours writing. Yet he, like Anthony, is also a victim of his illusions and vulnerable to society's allurements. Very early in the novel Maury clearly evaluates the depth of Caramel's artistic character when he tells Anthony, "Dick doesn't necessarily see more than any one else. He merely can put down a larger proportion of what he sees" (20). Confronted with the possibility of becoming rich through his writings, Caramel compromises, nor does he foresee the weakness and consequences of his actions. By the end of *The Beautiful and Damned*, "It had become the custom among the young and clever reviewers to mention Richard Caramel with a smile of scorn. 'Mr.' Richard Caramel, they called him. His corpse was dragged obscenely through every literary supplement. He was accused of making a great fortune by writing trash for the movies. As the fashion in books shifted he was becoming almost a byword of contempt" (422). Both Dick and Anthony are characters who have allowed their desires to become self-destructive. They are also unaware of their damnation and the essential part each played in it. Caramel at the end of *The Beautiful and Damned* tells his depressed and alcoholic friend Anthony, " 'I'm sick of all this shoddy realism. I think there's a place for the romanticist in literature' " (421).

Almost all the characters in *The Beautiful and Damned* share Caramel's sentiment that there is no place for them in an American society that lacked, in Mencken's words, "a civilized aristocracy" or whose aristocracy consisted of reformers like Adam Patch, a millionaire with "the bad temper of a spoiled child" and a "fatuous desire for a land of harps and canticles on earth" (15). The one exception is a social outsider, Joseph Bloeckman, a successful Jewish movie producer. His life, as Fitzgerald describes it, has overtones of the Horatio Alger myth:

> Born in Munich he had begun his American career as a peanut vendor with a travelling circus. At eighteen he was a side show ballyhoo; later, the manager of the side show, and, soon after, the proprietor of a second-class vaudeville house. Just when the moving picture had passed out of the stage of a curiosity and become a promising industry he was an ambitious young man of twenty-six with some money to invest, nagging financial ambitions and a good working knowledge of the popular show business. That had been nine years before. The moving picture industry had borne him up with it where it threw off dozens of men with more financial ability, more imagination, and more practical ideas . . . (96–7)

Bloeckman at one point had courted Gloria, but she had refused his offer of marriage in favour of Anthony. More than that she had often ridiculed and treated him as an uncouth inferior. At first Anthony is shocked at Gloria's behaviour, but soon after he treats him the same way. In their eyes this successful Jew has become the symbol of their contempt for all the stupid, unsophisticated Americans who aspire to become aristocrats, a contempt saturated with racism. *The Beautiful and Damned* is amply laced with nasty remarks about the lower classes, Jews, Italians, Negroes, "Millions of people," as Gloria says, "swarming like rats, chattering like apes, smelling like all hell . . . monkeys! Or lice, I suppose" (394).

Fitzgerald does not endorse this racism. As Anthony and Gloria deteriorate, Bloeckman becomes more wealthy and sophisticated. The scene at the end of the novel where Anthony, drunk and broken, insults Bloeckman and this time is beaten up, is Fitzgerald's final judgment on racism and Bloeckman's character. Yet this proud movie producer plays a more significant role in the scheme of the novel. He is a subtle mirror of Anthony's deep sense of inferiority which is also a dimension of his romantic longings for the realm of ideal beauty and safety. Bloeckman has accomplished by hard work what Anthony, immersed in passivity, cannot. At the end of *The Beautiful and Damned* both Anthony and Gloria are for a time as hopelessly dependent upon Bloeckman for their existence as they are upon the money of Adam Patch.

Salvation and identity finally arrive for Anthony and Gloria. After a long drawn-out lawsuit contesting the will, they are awarded thirty million dollars. When last seen aboard *The Berengaria* through the eyes of two disinterested fellow passengers, Anthony is broken mentally and physically and Gloria, wearing an expensive Russian sable coat, seems "sort of dyed and *unclean*" (448). Anthony's passive pursuit of an identity is over. But he is in no condition to feel a sense of fulfilment or remorse if the money fails to satisfy his intense longings. Ironically the person who profits most from Anthony's quest is Gloria, whose overpowering beauty and vitality he once believed would be the sources of his identity.

When, five years before, feeling self-divided and lonely, Anthony had entertained Gloria, "The Beautiful Lady", and her cousin Maury in the elegant safety of his New York apartment, Gloria's beauty had immediately overwhelmed him.

121

She was dazzling—alight; it was agony to comprehend her beauty in a glance. Her hair, full of a heavenly glamour, was gay against the winter color of the room. . . .

He saw, at length, that her eyes were gray, very level and cool, and when they rested on him he understood what Maury had meant by saying she was very young and very old. She talked always about herself as a very charming child might talk, and her comments on her tastes and distastes were unaffected and spontaneous. (57–60)

Blinded by infatuation for this woman Anthony had attempted a fusion with this beauty through marriage. For most adolescents intimacy of any kind is a threat. Lacking a firm self-delineation, they look upon any close love relationship as "an interpersonal fusion amounting to a loss of identity".[16] But Anthony is not afraid of fusion, he had longed for it. He had longed for a woman with the power to make him whole and give him a new self, a firm identity. He had been lifeless and Gloria was "a sun, radiant, growing, gathering light and storing it—then after an eternity pouring it forth in a glance, the fragment of a sentence, to that part of him that cherished all beauty and all illusion" (73). Anthony clearly was not seeking that true intimacy, "a counterpointing as well as a fusing of identities". He had yearned, rather, for relief from his incomplete, conflicted self, "for rest in her great immobility" and fusion with her beauty which he believes means "the end of all restlessness, all malcontent" (107).

Anthony's ten week romance with Gloria had ended in marriage but not before Gloria had deprived Anthony of what little dignity he possessed. Still her cruelty did not frustrate his desires because the forces of Gloria's beauty and childlike youth penetrated Anthony's defences and merged with the emotional sources of his "nostalgia for a lost paradise".

After about a year of marriage the glow of infatuation and novelty had disappeared. Gloria discovered that Anthony was weak, fearful, and restless. Anthony found Gloria's beauty and teasing less attractive hiding, as it did, the other Gloria Gilbert whom Richard Lehan describes as "the slightly schizophrenic girl who moves between states of exaggerated excitement and melancholy pouting".[17] Their original love deteriorated into lethargy, and while they awaited the verdict about the will, they came to hate each other bitterly. Yet they had remained together, well aware that their youth and beauty were failing, still hopeful of one day being transformed by Adam Patch's wealth.

At the end of the book the reasons for their union are far from ideal and optimistic. Gloria, egocentric, careless, and pleasure seeking, believes that money will restore or replace her fading beauty and youth which were the foundations of her irresponsible exciting lifestyle before marriage. For Anthony Gloria has long since lost the power to make him whole. As in Gatsby's relationship with Daisy, the ultimate question here is not what Anthony sees in Gloria, but what she represents. To a lonely man she still mirrors those romantic yearnings which have always guided his way of life, and he still believes she has the power to save him and give him an identity. The supreme irony of *The Beautiful and Damned* is that when salvation comes, it finds Anthony, as he had always been, psychologically unprepared to embrace the good fortune of his salvation. He is thus left damned to continue his life without an authentic identity. Doubtless in Fitzgerald's eyes Anthony was doomed to such a state of loss even if he had possessed his sanity and his wealth at the same time. For the good in Anthony's life always remained in his vision and in his struggle, not in the forms of fulfilment he chose.

NOTES

1   Erikson, *Identity*, p. 40.
2   *The Eccentric Design: Form in the Classic American Novel* (New York: Columbia University Press, 1963), p. 265.
3   Marius Bewley, "Great Scott", *New York Review of Books*, 16 September 1965, p. 23.
4   "Scott Fitzgerald—the Authority of Failure", in *F. Scott Fitzgerald*, ed. Arthur M. Mizener (Englewood Cliffs, N.J.: Prentice-Hall, 1963), p. 21.
5   Richard D. Lehan, *F. Scott Fitzgerald and the Craft of Fiction* (Carbondale: Southern Illinois University Press, 1966), p. 38.
6   F. Scott Fitzgerald, *The Beautiful and Damned* (New York: Scribner's, 1922), p. 126. All further quotations are from this edition; page reference will be indicated after the quotation.
7   *The Eccentric Design*, p. 266.
8   *F. Scott Fitzgerald: His Art and His Technique*, p. 82.
9   Erikson, *Identity*, p. 101.
10 Erikson, *Identity*, p. 99.
11 Erikson, *Identity*, p. 88.

12 Erikson, *Identity*, p. 132.
13 Fitzgerald, *Letters*, p. 163.
14 Sklar, p. 96.
15 Mizener, p. 130.
16 Erikson, *Identity*, p. 167.
17 Lehan, p. 80.

5

The Great Gatsby: Jay Gatsby

While writing *The Great Gatsby* in 1924 Fitzgerald had something of a struggle with the character of Gatsby. At one point, as he wrote Maxwell Perkins, he was tempted "to let him go and have Tom Buchanan dominate the book" thinking Buchanan was the best character he had ever created. Fitzgerald, however, dropped this idea when he rediscovered the power of the character. As he revealed to Perkins, "Gatsby sticks in my heart, I had him for awhile, then lost him, and now I know I have him again". Although Fitzgerald was aware of the practical disadvantages of writing "a man's book", *The Great Gatsby*, as he said, "contains no important woman character and women control the fiction market at present",[1] this did not prevent him from finally creating, with Perkins's help, Jay Gatsby, a mythic figure whose presence has the emotional force to dominate a novel filled with marvellously palpable and vital characters.

The psychological resistances Fitzgerald encountered while creating Gatsby are not surprising, since Gatsby embodied so many of the most painful experiences, fears, and desires of Fitzgerald's own life. At the end of 1924 Fitzgerald told Perkins, "I know Gatsby better than I know my own child". Several months after *Gatsby* was published Fitzgerald confessed to John Peale Bishop that his own countenance was behind the mask of Jay Gatsby who, as Fitzgerald wrote, "started as one man I knew and then changed into myself—the amalgam was never complete in my mind."[2] What Fitzgerald meant, Henry Dan Piper maintains, "was not his literal, but rather his moral countenance",[3] one that was primarily fashioned by the author's sense of Roman Catholicism. *The Great Gatsby* is a religious work, a moral fable, because it is grounded in a structure of intensely ambivalent religious emotions. These religious considerations, which formed the basis for Gatsby's

125

amoral idealism and Nick's moral judgment, are the topic of Fitzgerald's short story, "Absolution". Written in 1922 the story was
originally to be the prologue of *The Great Gatsby*, but was later
discarded when Fitzgerald decided to approach the novel "from
a new angle". He had intended the story to be a picture of Gatsby's
early life but left it out to preserve the tight form and sense of
mystery of the novel. Yet, no matter what Fitzgerald's reasons were
for the exclusion of "Absolution", it still remains an extremely
valuable story without which any criticism of *The Great Gatsby*,
especially a psychological study of its main character, would be
incomplete.

"Absolution", as Piper characterizes it, "is the story of an eleven-
year-old boy's first encounter with evil".[4] The controlling external
forces in the lonely life of Fitzgerald's intense adolescent hero,
Rudolph Miller, are the Catholic Church, represented by Father
Schwartz, and his parents, ineffectual and frustrated middle-aged
people. Father Schwartz, an incurable romantic who is "unable to
attain a complete mystical union with our Lord",[5] weeps "cold
tears" in the still of the night. During the "hot madness" of a
Dakota day, aroused by the shrill laughter of Swedish girls and
"the scent of cheap toilet soap", the sexually deprived priest con-
jures up images of a more satisfying existence in a magical world
governed by his fantasy that "when a whole lot of people get together in the best places things go glimmering all the time" (149).

Neither of Rudolph's parents has a strong sense of individual
identity or shares a mutual bond of intimacy. The father, Carl
Miller, as an energetic young man, had once believed that he lived
in a land of great opportunities—but that was twenty years ago.
"Absolution" presents him as a freight-agent resigned to failure
because he is "insufficiently hard-headed and unable to take fundamental relationships for granted, and this inability made him
suspicous, unrestful, and continually dismayed" (142). Yet, like
Father Schwartz, this constricted, angry man silently fantasizes
about "the colorful life" in two heavens, one on earth ruled by
the Empire Builder, James J. Hill, the other, eternal and Roman
Catholic, tyrannized by a wrathful God. For twenty years these
alone have been the principal sources of Carl Miller's personal
identity and behaviour.

There are only two sentences in "Absolution" about Rudolph
Miller's mother. They very deftly characterize her as an ageing,

nervous, ineffectual woman ill-equipped by nature or her marriage to be a trusting mother. Although she tries to be of some comfort to her son as he cries in pain from the physical punishment he has received from his father, Rudolph despises his mother's general weakness and rejects her attempts to aid him. She, like her husband and son, is an isolate in the Miller house. Her husband, incapable of human intimacy, does not share a bed with her. Father and son go off to church without her. Rudolph rejects not only her touch but also the fact that she is his real mother. Her identity as a wife and mother is indeed nominal. She appears destined to remain a lonely, unfulfilled woman.

Victimized by a sterile, severely religious homelife and tormented by awakening sexual desires, the adolescent Rudolph secretly creates a make-believe playmate, Blatchford Sarnemington, who embodies everything the lonely Rudolph is not and wants to be. Most of all, as an alter ego, Blatchford soars above all earthly laws of good and evil, responsible only to one god—his imagination. When Rudolph commits a wrong he immediately pretends that it is not Rudolph who has sinned, but Blatchford. This fantasy, however, is usually short-lived and soon disintegrates before Rudolph's precocious Catholic conscience.

Such is the case one Saturday afternoon when, after anxiously confessing to Father Schwartz his usual list of sins (mostly sexual, and thereby surviving "another crisis in his religious life") Rudolph believes he can introduce some joy into the confessional, "that large coffin set on end", by dramatically assuring the priest he never tells lies. At first Rudolph glories in the brilliance of his performance, but before long his conscience asserts itself. Rudolph knows he has often told lies and realizes that his brilliant performance has led him to commit the terrible sin of telling a falsehood during confession. At first he pretends Blatchford is responsible for the lie, but the imaginary playmate proves too insubstantial against the desperate force of conscience. Unable to resolve the predicament in his imagination, and caught between his father's dominating religiosity and the shameful prospect of having to go to confession again to confess his new terrible sin, Rudolph reacts by deliberately receiving Holy Communion in a state of mortal sin thereby blackening his soul even more.

After several terrifying days filled with thoughts of a vengeful God about to strike him dead because of the "black poison he carried in his heart", Rudolph goes to Father Schwartz and confesses everything. Instead of granting absolution to the penitent, the priest sees his own frustrations and longings in Rudolph's defiant gestures, condones them, and frantically tells the boy about his own wild dreams of seeing life as a glittering amusement park to which you "don't get up close" (150). Fitzgerald's brilliant counterpointing in this scene of a frustrated and an innocent imagination reveals how the seeds of religious doubt are planted in Rudolph's mind. Confronted with Father Schwartz's half-crazed talk of a glimmering world beyond God, family, and fears, Rudolph senses the truth of his own romantic imagination—there is a realm in which he can be free to exist forever as Blatchford Sarnemington. Although the young boy finally runs in panic from the rectory

> . . . underneath his terror he felt that his own inner convictions were confirmed. There was something ineffably gorgeous somewhere that had nothing to do with God. He no longer thought that God was angry at him about the original lie, because He must have understood that Rudolph had done it to make things finer in the confessional, brightening up the dinginess of his admissions by saying a thing radiant and proud. At the moment when he had affirmed immaculate honor a silver pennon had flapped out into the breeze somewhere and there had been the crunch of leather and the shine of silver spurs and a troop of horsemen waiting for dawn on a low green hill. (150)

"Absolution" is Fitzgerald's celebration of the vast creative power of the imagination. In this story he has replaced the imagination's conventional goals—fame, money and the beautiful girl—with the possibility that Rudolph's romantic imagination might entertain God Himself. Such a sense of pride and responsibility projects the young hero into a world much more satisfying than the one governed by his ineffectual parents and the frightening demands of Roman Catholicism. By transforming himself into Blatchford, Rudolph discards his human past, deliberately assuming a new identity "safe from God" where in the past he had prepared the "subterfuges with which he often tricked God" (141). Rudolph's assumption of such an extreme degree of romantic idealism by its very nature cannot fail to end in disillusionment and defeat. At the age of eleven he has already charted the course of his identity that will lead him in *The Great Gatsby* to West Egg.

Although Fitzgerald considered "Absolution", which appeared in the June 1922 issue of *American Mercury*, and *The Great Gatsby*, published on 10 April 1925, as separate works with different characters, it is critically justifiable to use the short story as an imaginary prologue to the novel. "Absolution" is based upon material cut out of *Gatsby*, and Fitzgerald made it clear that he intended the story to be a picture of Gatsby's early life. Therefore one may look upon Rudolph Miller as a legitimate precursor to Jay Gatsby. In the novel Rudolph is Jimmie Gatz while Blatchford Sarnemington officially emerges as Jay Gatsby when at seventeen Jimmie Gatz sees "Dan Cody's yacht drop anchor over the most insidious flat on Lake Superior"[6] and decides to change his name.

There Gatsby assumes for five years the position of steward and guardian of Dan Cody, "a gray, florid man with a hard, empty face—the pioneer debauchee, who during one phase of American life brought back to the Eastern seaboard the savage violence of the frontier brothel and saloon" (101). During this time Gatsby matures in the ways of the material world. Still he retains the belief "that the rock of the world was founded securely on a fairy's wing" (100) because his career began with Jimmie's decision to change his name. Furthermore, as Henry Piper perceptively explains, "that career began, as we know from 'Absolution', when eleven-year-old Jimmie Gatz decided to commit himself to the moral world of his own imagination—a world where he could be 'safe from God' ".[7] With this decision Jimmie Gatz had already stripped himself of the past, the roots and history of his identity and given birth to a new romantic self, Jay Gatsby:

> His parents were shiftless and unsuccessful farm people—his imagination had never really accepted them as his parents at all. The truth was that Jay Gatsby of West Egg, Long Island, sprang from his Platonic conception of himself. He was a son of God—a phrase which, if it means anything, means just that —and he must be about His Father's business, the service of a vast, vulgar, and meretricious beauty. So he invented just the sort of Jay Gatsby that a seventeen-year-old boy would be likely to invent, and to this conception he was faithful to the end. (99)

There are elements of grandeur and immaturity in Gatsby's vision of himself. Both of these characteristics can be traced back to the religious considerations Fitzgerald dramatized in "Absolution". Gatsby's romanticism, a product of the spirit, is relentlessly optimistic in its quest for fulfilment within a materialistic society that denies the power of the spirit and offers instead the limitless material, and therefore exhaustible, possibilities of success, money, and romance. It energetically believes in the goodness of nature, man, and the present life and rejects all forms of limit, all the implications of the Christian view of man's imperfect nature. Like Anthony Patch in Fitzgerald's *The Beautiful and Damned*, perpetual youth and beauty of the body and spirit are essential requirements of Gatsby's belief in the infinite possibilities of American life. But at the heart of this compulsion, as Marius Bewley carefully points out, is "a promise rather than the possession of a vision, a faith in the half-glimpsed, but hardly understood, possibilities of life"[8] because Gatsby's materialistic America engenders extreme romantic desires but fails to offer heroic fulfilments.

Although Gatsby may die of "a love for which there is no worthy object",[9] the grandeur of his vision remains. It manifests itself in the rare quality of his faith in the goodness of creation and in his ultimate, although only partially recognized, refusal to compromise with the "colossal vitality" of his dream. Gatsby possesses an almost limitless sense of generosity. He yearns to give meaning to the lives of others and invest the world with his qualities of faith and hope in the infinite resources of his own imagination. Nick recognizes these rare aspirations that hide behind Gatsby's "unbroken series of successful gestures" the first time they meet.

"I'm Gatsby," he said suddenly.

"What!" I exclaimed. "Oh, I beg your pardon."

"I thought you knew, old sport. I'm afraid I'm not a very good host."

He smiled understandingly—much more than understandingly. It was one of those rare smiles with a quality of eternal reassurance in it, that you may come across four or five times in life. It faced—or seemed to face—the whole external world for an instant, and then concentrated on *you* with an irresistible prejudice in your favor. It understood you just as far as you wanted to be understood, believed in you as you would like to believe in yourself, and assured you that it had precisely the impression of you that, at your best, you hoped to convey. Precisely at that point it vanished—and I was looking at an elegant young rough-neck, a year or two over thirty, whose elaborate formality of speech just missed being absurd. (48)

As a romantic personality Gatsby transcends the limits of the Jazz Age and, as Marius Bewley rightfully declares, emerges as a "mythic character" expressing the destinies, aspirations, and attitudes of Western Man.[10] Although Gatsby's quest leads him into a vast material wilderness of illusions, he still retains the traditional legacy of the eternal promises of his Catholic upbring-ing in his misdirected search for transcendence amid the material promises of the American dream. Psychologically, he cannot shed the basic image of Rudolph Miller, a youth searching for a glimpse of God beyond the harsh commands of a father and irrational words of a frustrated priest.

Unfortunately Gatsby never recognizes the grandeur or the immaturity of his romantic vision. He never completely sees through the ultimate limitations of his aspirations. In any vision of the world man is always subject to time and mutability. But when an individual like Gatsby strives on earth for an ideal world of youth and beauty that is beyond time, he is both overwhelmed and damned. Fitzgerald, unlike Gatsby, knew that man was always engaged in a struggle with time and decay. One could never arrest the passage of youth, sustain an idealized moment of love forever or repeat the past. Failing to realize the destructiveness of time, Gatsby tries to live in a world where past, present, and future are all one. The ultimate result of his effort is "unutterable depres-sion" and failure—a "walk up and down a desolate path of fruit rinds and discarded favors and crushed flowers" (111).

Gatsby's vision also suffers from a form of moral myopia. He does not recognize the speciousness of the world of the very rich where he searched for fulfilment. He fails to see that the Buch-anans, representative of a class with its origins and ways of life nourished by wealth, are sordid and spiritually barren yet extremely powerful. Tom's "hard malice" and Daisy's carelessness easily destroy Gatsby's vulgar romanticism and leave him helpless but not ultimately corrupted. The root of Gatsby's distorted view is the failure of a traditional sense of self-knowledge and human im-perfection and mortality that would have been the basis of a more critical and secure grasp of social and human values. Without

131

this discriminating measure the dreams of a romantic idealist are doomed. Gatsby is defeated externally in his quest for his identity, a dream of love, by evil, incarnated in the organized forces of Tom and Daisy Buchanan and the other seductive traps of American society. But more significantly, he defeats himself internally because he lacks a firmly developed set of moral standards whereby to judge the limitations of his quest for love and "what foul dust floated in the wake of his dreams . . ."(2).

Jay Gatsby, whom Fitzgerald labelled a "crook" and a "parvenu", seems unaware of the essential fact that he is as ruthless and amoral with his vision as the Buchanans are with their money. Early in life he succeeds in creating a glittering new identity, but in the process Jay Gatsby abandons the fundamental moral heritage reflected in Rudolph Miller's Catholic childhood, a heritage based on the perception of man's imperfection and mortality which might have saved him from the emotional extremes of his idealizing self and the careless world of the Buchanans. In *The Great Gatsby* Fitzgerald bestows the invaluable product of this heritage upon the narrator Nick Carraway. Nick possesses a sturdy set of ethical norms based upon an awareness of death[11] that manifests itself in the ability to be "within and without, simultaneously enchanted and repelled by the inexhaustible variety of life" (36). This enables Nick to sympathize deeply with Jay Gatsby, and at the same time incisively judge the moral value of Gatsby's goals and methods. Nick can gaze in envious wonder across the bay at the "white palaces of fashionable East Egg" (5) among which was "a cheerful red-and-white Georgian Colonial mansion" (6) belonging to the wealthy and socially elite Buchanans, can live in their apparently golden world for a time, and still can clearly recognize that behind Tom Buchanan's enormous wealth, there festered an aggressive arrogance, a cruel will to power, and a deep urge to dominate and treat everyone with "paternal contempt". Likewise, he could perceive that behind Daisy's lovely, bright face, low, thrilling voice, and flattering personality that seemed to tell everyone she met that "there was no one in the world she so much wanted to see" (9), there rankled a "basic insincerity", contemptuous selfishness, and a corroding cynicism that "asserted her membership in a rather distinguished secret society to which she and Tom belonged" (18).

At the end of *The Great Gatsby* Nick Carraway applies this

strong sense of moral knowledge to the people and experiences he encounters in the dazzling East even though he too, like Gatsby, had come East from the Middle West that "seemed like the ragged edge of the universe" (3) to seek his fortune. This invaluable consciousness of the fundamental virtues, "honor, courtesy, and courage", finally saves Nick from following in the footsteps of the tragic Jay Gatsby or the careless Tom and Daisy Buchanan and sends him back to the Middle West of his father, the leader of the Carraway clan. From his father Nick had received this saving heritage of traditional moral values. The value that he placed upon this paternal gift is evident from his first words as he starts to narrate his story of Jay Gatsby.

> In my younger and more vulnerable years my father gave me some advice that I've been turning over in my mind ever since.
>
> "Whenever you feel like criticizing any one," he told me, "just remember that all the people in this world haven't had the advantages that you've had."
>
> He didn't say any more, but we've always been unusually communicative in a reserved way, and I understood that he meant a great deal more than that. In consequence, I'm inclined to reserve all judgments. . . . Reserving judgments is a matter of infinite hope. I am still a little afraid of missing something if I forget that, as my father snobbishly suggested, and I snobbishly repeat, a sense of the fundamental decencies is parcelled out unequally at birth. (1)

These words embody the picture of a father who has certainly passed on to his son a set of durable ethical norms necessary for a mature identity. But of more importance is the fact that Nick realizes their ultimate value and tries to judge his experiences according to these honourable imperatives.

On the basis of the earlier story "Absolution" we can see that Jay Gatsby was far less fortunate with his parents than Nick. Fitzgerald's presentation of parental figures in The Great Gatsby is basically consistent with that of the earlier story, but before returning to "Absolution" as the richer source of evidence for Gatsby's childhood let us look at the evidence we have from the novel. Fitzgerald makes no mention whatsoever of Gatsby's mother and does not introduce his father until after Gatsby's death when Henry C. Gatz arrives from a town in Minnesota.

. . . a solemn old man, very helpless and dismayed, bundled up in a long cheap ulster against the warm September day. His eyes leaked continuously with excitement, and when I took the bag and umbrella from his hands he began to pull so incessantly at his sparse gray beard that I had difficulty in getting off his coat. He was on the point of collapse, so I took him into the music room and made him sit down while I sent for something to eat. But he wouldn't eat, and the glass of milk spilled from his trembling hand. (167–8)

This is Fitzgerald's verbal portrait-painting at its best. Through the author's precise focusing upon the most seemingly common yet concretely poetic detail or action, Mr. Gatz comes alive like the other active minor characters in the novel, Myrtle Wilson, Meyer Wolfsheim and Klipspringer.

The father seems to consider himself a success as a parent. He is proud of his son. The splendour of Gatsby's huge house fills him with "an awed pride", and he compares him to the well-known Midwestern railroad tycoon who was also Carl Miller's idol. "If he'd of lived, he'd of been a great man. A man like James J. Hill. He'd of helped build up the country" (169). Mr. Gatz, like his son, believes that money and notoriety are the gauges of success. Ironically he even pulls out a ragged old copy of a book called *Hopalong Cassidy* and shows Nick the back cover where there appears young Gatsby's schedule for "success", a rigid formula reminiscent of the writings in Benjamin Franklin's *Poor Richard's Almanac* which often stressed the essential importance of self-improvement and hard work if one is to succeed in America. In his own way Henry Gatz, who journeyed East for Gatsby's funeral, is as morally blind as his son and could not possibly have provided Gatsby with any solid moral vision.

At the end of *The Great Gatsby* Nick realizes that "this has been a story of the West, after all—Tom and Gatsby, Daisy and Jordan and I, were all Westerners, and perhaps we possessed some deficiency in common which made us subtly unadaptable to Eastern life" (177). Nick is right about their showing a common weakness, one that was more personal than social. But each still possessed his or her own private Western backgrounds and deficiencies. For Gatsby's undoubtedly was the guilt-ridden Dakota world of Roman Catholicism and sensuous Swedish girls where in the earlier Fitzgerald short story Rudolph Miller was born and raised by unhappy parents living in a state of fear and mutual frustration.

Rudolph Miller's first meeting with this Western world in the person of his nervously ineffectual mother planted in him a sense of basic mistrust. This radical impairment, according to Erik Erikson, leaves the child with strong feelings of estrangement. He does not experience himself as separate, genuine, and the possessor of an inner consistency but is drawn to two or more selves.[12] Such a schizoid personality grounded Rudolph's earliest interactions with himself and others and continued to motivate his behaviour even after he committed himself at eleven years of age to imaginatively refashioning his life by casting off the experiences and effects of an oppressive childhood. Moreover, Rudolph's deliberate disruption of his personality intensified the earlier schizoid feelings of mistrust and inner division by widening the gap between his original self and his ideal self, Blatchford Sarnemington.

For most Freudians, like Erikson, orality is the mark of the schizoid. Since Fitzgerald, a novelist so dependent for his material upon personal experience, suspiciously neglected the thorough examination of the mother figure in his writings with the possible exception of Beatrice in *This Side of Paradise* (Fitzgerald never resolved his feelings of hostility and guilt towards his own eccentric mother), we can also derive Rudolph's defective resolution of his primary crisis of trust manifested by multiple selves from Gatsby's excessive orality and sense of nostalgia.

Freud first devised the concept of an oral character, such as Gatsby, in order to explain the seemingly random personality traits of his adult patients. He theorized that later human behaviour derives from earlier childhood trauma and unsolved conflicts experienced during the oral stage when Erikson believes basic trust must establish and maintain itself. Freud and later analysts like Erikson traced adult symptoms to serious problems during the early months of the primary relationship between a troubled mother and hungry child whom she feeds but also terrifies or frustrates in the process. A history was therefore given to the symptoms and the term "oral character" was increasingly used to describe, as Robert Coles writes, "a person who shows in his behavior, in his cravings, his tight-lipped stability, his asceticism, his overindulgence in food or drink or tobacco, consistent evidence that what happened in his mother's arms or in the high chair meant enough in the past to persist in the present as an 'attitude' or even as a whole way of life".[13]

Normal orality usually "expresses itself in our dependencies and nostalgias, and in our all too hopeful and all too hopeless states".[14] There are, however, two forms of pronounced orality that oftentimes in varying degrees coexist in the same person. Excessive oral satisfaction during a child's earliest months results in strong self-assurance and optimism which may continue throughout his life. Exceptional oral deprivation, in turn, is the cause of an individual's pessimistic or sadistic attitude. Whenever either of these two extreme forms of early orality becomes dominant, infantile fears later manifest themselves in a need for the optimistic oral character, as Erikson points out, "to make giving and receiving the most important thing in life" and for the pessimistic or sadistic oral character "to get and to take in ways harmful to others or to oneself".[15] In either of those cases the oral character is dependent on people and objects for the maintenance of self-esteem. Although this type of person may appear entirely independent and unconcerned, excessive emotional and material generosity or niggardliness indicate unsolved conflicts during his oral stage and a deep need for approval and security because of a weak identity.

On the most obvious level Gatsby's form of optimistic orality may be seen in his role and reputation as an extravagant party host. Through the summer nights fantastic yet vulgar parties take place on Gatsby's estate to which a "menagerie" of people come uninvited. They thoughtlessly make use of his house and private beach and feast upon a wide variety of expensive foods from "buffet tables, garnished with glistening hors-d'oeuvre, spiced baked hams crowded against salads of harlequin designs and pastry pigs and turkeys bewitched to a dark gold" (39–40). Later the centre of the party shifts to the main hall where "a bar with a real brass rail was set up, and stocked with gins and liquors and with cordials so long forgotten that most of his female guests were too young to know one from another" (40).

These guests, who perform "according to the rules of behavior associated with amusement parks" (41), are stimulated by the mysterious past and present occupation of their unknown host. They thrill to unreliable and often unsavoury stories about Gatsby. One reports "somebody told me they thought he killed a man once". Another thinks "it's more that he was a German spy during the war" (44). Among such rumours there is one factual story about Gatsby's notorious generosity recounted by Lucille, a frequent uninvited partier:

> "When I was here last I tore my gown on a chair, and he asked me my name and address—inside of a week I got a package from Croirier's with a new evening gown in it."
> "Did you keep it?" asked Jordan.
> "Sure I did. I was going to wear it tonight, but it was too big in the bust and had to be altered. It was gas blue with lavender beads. Two hundred and sixty-five dollars." (43)

No one except Nick knows that the motive for Gatsby's generosity and elaborate display of wealth is the unrealistic hope that Daisy will somehow appear at one of his parties, be pleased by the pageant she sees, and wish to renew her love affair with him. Gatsby thinks of his material possessions, not himself, as the most powerful means of regaining Daisy. Gatsby's obsessive longing to recreate the past, to win back Daisy, is his most intense manifestation of orality. Lacking a sense of basic trust, Gatsby as an infant was afflicted with an unusually acute sense of loss, in Erikson's words, "a universal nostalgia for a lost paradise", the effect of which is a strong orally sadistic yearning to merge into a larger identity later represented by the beautiful and wealthy Daisy Fay.

When Gatsby is an Army officer stationed in Louisville, Kentucky, he accidentally meets Daisy, "the first 'nice' girl he had ever known" (148). Blinded by his all-consuming need for identity and completeness Gatsby, making use of false social pretences, "took Daisy one still October night, took her because he had no real right to touch her hand" (149). He had intended to take what he could and leave. Instead Gatsby found himself committed "to the following of a grail" (149) because Daisy was an extraordinary, "nice girl" who lived a rich, full life and could vanish into a rich house depriving him, a handsome but poor young man, of the identity, love, and inner security he had never possessed but now longed for even more since he had experienced their pleasures through her.

Most insecure adolescents feel, like Gatsby, endangered by intimacy, believing any close love relationship is, as Erikson says, "an interpersonal fusion amounting to a loss of identity".[16] Gatsby longs for such a fusion with Daisy. His goal is not true intimacy but the sense of a perfectly satisfying identity since it is a traditional and widely followed American cultural conviction that the possession of a beautiful woman is one of the signs of personal fulfilment. The strong verbal influence of John Keats shines through Fitzgerald's richly poetic description of Gatsby's emotional marriage to Daisy:

> . . . they had been walking down the street when the leaves were falling, and they came to a place where there were no trees and the sidewalk was white with moonlight. They stopped here and turned toward each other. Now it was a cool night with that mysterious excitement in it which comes at the two changes of the year. The quiet lights in the houses were humming out into the darkness and there was a stir and bustle among the stars. Out of the corner of his eye Gatsby saw that the blocks of the sidewalks really formed a ladder and mounted to a secret place above the trees—he could climb to it, if he climbed alone, and once there he could suck on the pap of life, gulp down the incomparable milk of wonder.
>
> His heart beat faster and faster as Daisy's white face came up to his own. He knew that when he kissed this girl, and forever wed his unutterable visions to her perishable breath, his mind would never romp again like the mind of God. So he waited, listening for a moment longer to the tuning-fork that had been struck upon a star. Then he kissed her. At his lips' touch she blossomed for him like a flower and the incarnation was complete. (112)

Gatsby's past and future merge in this moment of commitment when, as Richard Lehan indicates, "his conception of beauty was fixed, and his will yearned eternally for that beauty".[17] But, more significantly, the graphic images of orality in this passage suggest the deeper source of Gatsby's transcendent longings for Daisy, his insecure, love-starved childhood. The conditions of Gatsby's childhood deprivations and his fear of losing Daisy aggravated by his "nostalgia for a lost paradise", may be discerned in the extreme quality of his oral sadism, the need to identify completely with, and even consume, Daisy, the person by whom Gatsby wishes to be fed and satisfied. Orally sadistic characters, like Gatsby, according to Otto Fenichel, "request and demand a great deal, will not relinquish their object and affix themselves by

138

'suction' ".[18] Oftentimes their oral-sadistic tendencies are vampire-like in character, harmful to both themselves and their loved ones. This quality of oral-sadism to a great extent colours Gatsby's relentless, uncritical pursuit of Daisy. Unfortunately, Gatsby never fully realized the psychological complexity and limitless thrust of his aspirations. They soared beyond material possessions and the acquisition of Daisy. The loss of Daisy revived Gatsby's earliest crisis of trust, the effects of which shaped his development throughout the following stages of life. Since incorporation was Gatsby's primary form of oral behaviour, a need "to go and get" dictated the style of his growth through the closely related areas of autonomy, initiative, and industry. But any achievement in these areas was generally motivated by the will of others since the young Gatsby lacked a sense of trust in himself to be capable of making close, independent decisions. Gatsby's quest for Daisy replicated this childhood pattern of behaviour. He compulsively amassed material possessions by working hard and taking daring and dangerous gambles. Yet the concrete expressions and methods Gatsby employed to reach the success that he believed would guarantee Daisy's return and his identity were controlled by his unqualified belief in the power of material possessions to satisfy every person's deepest desires.

Fitzgerald recognized both the inadequacy of Gatsby's goals and the grandeur of his romantic vision and pursuit. Significantly, our first glimpse of Gatsby at the end of Chapter One is related to the central symbol in the book, the green light at the end of Daisy's dock. This symbol occurs several times throughout the novel. As Marius Bewley rightly says, "the whole being of Gatsby exists only in relation to what the green light symbolizes".[19] At the beginning of The Great Gatsby its primary function is to focus Gatsby's romantic vision upon Daisy. Under this form the green light against the background of a vast, formless body of water represents a beautiful woman, an embodiment of the glamour of wealth, whose possession will be the vital source of Gatsby's sense of identity and meaning in life. In particular the light's colour represents the wealth which Gatsby believed was the natural means whereby one purchases Daisy and the other magical material possessions necessary for identity and fulfilment.

Daisy, however, falls far short of Gatsby's imaginative expectations. After proudly showing her the material products of five years of work and patience, his mansion, "a colossal affair by any standard" (5), acres of gardens, dozens of shirts, they sit in the music-room listening to Klipspringer playing the piano. Outside the wind is loud and thunder flows along the Sound. "It was the hour of a profound human change, and excitement was generating on the air" (96). Inside, as Nick says, "There must have been moments even that afternoon when Daisy tumbled short of his dreams—not through her own fault, but because of the colossal vitality of his illusion. It had gone beyond her, beyond everything" (97). Gatsby's initial feelings of disillusionment are clearly not the product of his romance with Daisy; they are effects of his incapacity to compromise with the enormous demands of his inner vision that are bound to suffer from any contact with reality.

Although Daisy and the green light are no longer completely enchanted objects for Gatsby he will not give up the quest to recover that image of himself, his short-lived identity, that had gone into loving Daisy. In fact it becomes more intense and orally sadistic as he desperately tries to elevate the real Daisy to the exalted level and to create her in the image of his vision. Now Gatsby becomes truly the typical Fitzgerald hero, as defined by Richard Lehan, "a man of longing—whose very desires are self-destructive",[20] when he demands that Daisy help him to do the impossible; obliterate time and repeat the past. "He wanted nothing less of Daisy than that she should go to Tom and say: 'I never loved you.' After she had obliterated four years with that sentence they could decide upon the more practical measures to be taken. One of them was that, after she was free, they were to go back to Louisville and be married from her house—just as if it were five years ago" (111).

For Gatsby the years, his business activities, the wealth, house, parties, his social identity as a "Trimalchio", symbolized by the "desolate path of fruit rinds and discarded favors and crushed flowers" (111), had no meaning unless he could recover his vision of Daisy and himself in its godlike, immutable form. Jay Gatsby is as much an imaginative creation of James Gatz, as "Blatchford Sarnemington" was the creation of Rudolph Miller in "Absolution". As Robert Sklar points out, "Like Rudolph, Gatz was a lower-class young man whose imagination was so powerful that it leapt beyond his social and economic circumstances. Beyond, in origins, was 'his Platonic conception of himself,' a self-creative power that made him more powerful in his way than God, equal to God responsible to God. . . ."[21]

Gatsby, however, is so obsessed with his imaginative quest for Daisy, by which to confer an identity upon himself and reality upon the world, that he naïvely overlooks the power of Tom's "hard malice" and Daisy's amoral insincerity and carelessness. In the second half of the novel Gatsby's quest must contend with external forces represented by the callous and selfish social interests of the Buchanans. His orally sadistic quest is put to the acid test on a hot afternoon during August in "the parlor of a suite in the Plaza Hotel" (126) when Gatsby tries to make Daisy admit she never loved anyone except him.

> ". . . Just tell him [Tom] the truth—that you never loved him— and it's all wiped out forever!"
>
> She looked at him blindly. "Why—how could I love him— possibly?"
>
> "You never loved him."
>
> She hesitated. . . .
>
> "Oh, you want too much!" She cried to Gatsby. "I love you now—isn't that enough? I can't help what's past." She began to sob helplessly. "I did love him once—but I loved you too."
>
> Gatsby's eyes opened and closed.
>
> "You loved me *too*?" he repeated. (132–3)

The grandeur and excessive immaturity of Gatsby's yearnings are no match for the ruthless and amoral cruelty of Tom Buchanan, even though Gatsby himself had also made use of this same trait as he built up his fortune in such a short time. Before the afternoon slips away Gatsby finds himself fighting Tom and Daisy's organized forces with a "dead dream". His pursuit of Daisy and of his identity is over. His world of the green light is now "material without being real" (162). But the ultimate cause of Gatsby's defeat is not Tom or Daisy or the unlimited promises of material possessions but Gatsby himself, his vision of himself and the world. Gatsby asked too much of Daisy and the power of wealth because he lacked the basic trust needed to struggle with all the conflicting parts of himself and his past.

The primary question of *The Great Gatsby* is not the satisfying power of unlimited material possibilities or the character of Daisy. For Gatsby she "does not exist in herself. She is the green light that signals him into the heart of his ultimate vision."[22] It

is the sources in childhood of Gatsby's colossal faith in the goodness of life and his relentless quest to achieve all the possibilities
of existence. These sources, like his experiences with Daisy, lie
in the past, but in that part of the past which Gatsby believed
he had finally left behind—those lonely childhood days when he
was Jimmie Gatz, the son of rigidly Catholic parents, each of whom
lacked a sense of personal identity as a basis for mature fulfilment.
Only Gatsby in the novel believes a person can completely eliminate certain parts of one's past that are burdensome or useless and
imaginatively create one's self anew. Nick Carraway, the only
character in *The Great Gatsby* who sees Jay Gatsby for what he
really is, says that although Gatsby "represented everything for
which I have an unaffected scorn", nevertheless he alone possessed
"some heightened sensitivity to the promises of life . . . it was an
extraordinary gift for hope, a romantic readiness such as I have
never found in any other person and which it is not likely I shall
ever find again" (2).

Gatsby's romantic search for identity is characterized by the
belief that the world of his imagination is better by far than the
drab one ruled over by his parents and their Catholic religion.
This flight from a childhood past and subsequent commitment to
the power of romantic idealism is the source of Gatsby's heightened
sensitivity to the promises of life. It is also the cause of his admir-
able defeat. Gatsby failed to recognize that the past he tried to
escape from, especially the traditional values of Catholicism, represented in *The Great Gatsby* by Nick and the advice of his father,
could have saved him from himself and a society inhabited by
Buchanans which offers no commensurate objects for true heroic
desires.

Paradoxically, Gatsby's final fate is somewhat similar to those
of his parents. At the end of the novel, in spite of all his wealth
and possessions, Gatsby is alone and helpless while waiting in vain
for Daisy's phone call. As Nick says, "I have an idea that Gatsby
himself didn't believe it would come, and perhaps he no longer
cared" (162). The dream that gave meaning to his life has disappeared forever and with it his hopes for a true identity. His
faith in the possibilities of life, that "vast, vulgar, and meretricious
beauty", like his childhood faith in the God of Catholicism, has
been shattered. When death finally strikes Gatsby, as he lies on a
pneumatic mattress floating in his pool, he no longer possesses

"the old warm world" or the desire to be born anew. In Nick's words, "He must have looked up at an unfamiliar sky through frightening leaves and shivered as he found what a grotesque thing a rose is and how raw the sunlight was upon the scarcely created grass. A new world, material without being real, where poor ghosts, breathing dreams like air, drifted fortuitously about . . ." (162).

On the last page of *The Great Gatsby* Nick achieves the blending of Gatsby's dream and apparent failure with the aspirations of the historic American Dream of the early Dutch settlers in such beautifully universalizing terms that one loses sight of Gatsby and the psychological past that brought him to such a state of tragic helplessness.

> As the moon rose higher the inessential houses began to melt away until gradually I became aware of the old island here that flowered once for Dutch sailors' eyes—a fresh, green breast of the new world. Its vanished trees, the trees that had made way for Gatsby's house, had once pandered in whispers to the last and greatest of human dreams; for a transitory enchanted moment man must have held his breath in the presence of this continent. . . . (182)

Gatsby's imperishable dream repeats the pioneers' dream of creating a new life for themselves. In spite of all the richly evocative beauty of Nick's final words of hope from *The Great Gatsby*, one's deepest response to Gatsby's story is similar to that of a tragedy of great waste.

NOTES

1 Fitzgerald, *Letters*, p. 193.
2 Fitzgerald, *Letters*, p. 383.
3 *F. Scott Fitzgerald: A Critical Portrait*, p. 111.
4 Piper, p. 104.
5 F. Scott Fitzgerald, "Absolution", *Babylon Revisited and Other Stories* (New York: Scribner's, 1960), p. 136. All further quotations are from this edition; page reference will be indicated after the quotation.
6 F. Scott Fitzgerald, *The Great Gatsby* (New York: Scribner's, 1925), p. 98. All further quotations are from this edition; page reference will be indicated after the quotation.
7 Piper, pp. 105–6.
8 *Eccentric Design*, p. 270.

9 Marius Bewley, "Great Scott", p. 23.
10 *Eccentric Design*, p. 271.
11 Piper, pp. 107–8.
12 Erikson, *Identity*, p. 97.
13 *Erik H. Erikson: The Growth of His Work* (Boston: Atlantic-Little, Brown, 1970), p. 56.
14 Erikson, *Identity*, p. 102.
15 Erikson, *Identity*, p. 102.
16 Erikson, *Identity*, p. 167.
17 Lehan, p. 95.
18 *The Psychoanalytic Theory of Neurosis* (New York: Norton, 1945), p. 489.
19 *Eccentric Design*, p. 280.
20 Lehan, p. 38.
21 Sklar, p. 186.
22 *Eccentric Design*, p. 278.

6

Tender is the Night: Dick Diver

Scott Fitzgerald died with the conviction that *Tender is the Night* was his best book. "If you liked *The Great Gatsby*," he inscribed a copy of the novel for a friend, "for God's sake read this. Gatsby was a tour de force but this is a confession of faith."[1] Fitzgerald put into his last completed novel many of his wise and tragic beliefs about personal identity, the value of the traditional virtues— "honor, courtesy, courage", love, money, the dignity of work, material Fitzgerald found "so harrowing and highly charged" because it was the hard-earned product of years of painful and costly experiences.[2] Although *Tender is the Night* is the most autobiographical of Fitzgerald's works, he felt it had a universal attraction, "a novel", as he wrote John Peale Bishop, "that was inevitably close to whoever read it in my generation".[3]

Unfortunately, Fitzgerald was wrong about the wide popular and critical appeal of *Tender is the Night*. In 1934–1935 it sold 13,000 copies and was on the best-seller list for nine weeks. This kind of mass popularity was totally inadequate for Fitzgerald considering his standards and expectations. His self-confidence and capacity to go on as a serious writer depended upon the wide acceptance of the novel he called his "epic". Even more painful for the author to bear were the generally mixed reviews *Tender is the Night* received from the critics. Although John Peale Bishop, James Branch Cabell, and Morley Callaghan thought it was an outstanding advance over *The Great Gatsby*, most others including Ernest Hemingway, the contemporary writer Fitzgerald admired most, had major reservations with the subject matter and artistry. Objections to the book focused upon the credibility of Fitzgerald's group of self-indulgent expatriates, especially the main character Dick Diver, and the author's frequent and confusing shifts in point of view.

145

Fitzgerald realized the validity of both these criticisms. The distinct possibility of misleading readers into believing Rosemary Hoyt was the central character of *Tender is the Night* because of the emphasis put on her point of view in Book One disturbed Fitzgerald. Eventually he arranged the story in straight chronological order beginning with Dick Diver's personal history, this structure, as he wrote, being a part of "the final version of the book as I would like it".[4] Fitzgerald was also unmistakably aware of his failure to make Dick Diver's character psychologically coherent. Eight of the twenty-four original reviews of *Tender is the Night* criticized the credibility of Dick Diver, stressing the fact that his collapse seemed unconvincing or insufficiently documented.[5] Fitzgerald's subsequent decision to rearrange the novel's structure, the removal of the flashback and the placing of Dick's personal history first, was partially motivated by his desire to show that Diver's decline was the result of certain long-standing conflicts in his personality. This change, however, did not satisfy Fitzgerald. In 1939 he wrote Mrs. Edwin Jarrett who had written a stage adaptation of *Tender is the Night*, "I did not manage, I think in retrospect, to give Dick the cohesion I aimed at. . . . I wonder what the hell the first actor who played Hamlet thought of the part? I can hear him say, 'The guy's a nut, isn't he?' (We can always find great consolation in Shakespeare)."[6]

Even today after the careful and thorough re-examination of *Tender is the Night* that has caused a shift in interest and respect for the novel, there still remains a body of opinion—Otto Friedrich and Albert Lubell being the most articulate—which doubts the validity of Dick Diver's characterization. Although Fitzgerald never intended to write a novel specifically about a psychiatrist but about Dick Diver who is a psychiatrist, criticism is constantly made that Dick is not a persuasive figure as a psychiatrist. Many more informed readers find it hard to believe that anyone with Dick's medical training would so easily enter a marriage with a schizophrenic patient. As a psychiatrist Dick should have realized that a marriage based upon the transference of Nicole's affections was bound to end with the patient's return to health.

An even more controversial question still centres around the dominant reasons for Dick Diver's downfall. Most contemporary critics agree with James E. Miller when he says, "It is easy to blame the entirety of Dick's fall on the sophisticated cannibalism of the fabulous Warren world, so careless of other people's lives, or on the magnetic attraction of the fresh, young world of Rosemary Hoyt. But these answers are too simple; Dick's sickness lies hidden in lower depths than these."[7] Yet to say, as Miller does, that "a sinister kind of innocence that is debilitating in the face of evil"[8] is Dick's main psychological flaw, or to argue so eloquently, as Arthur Mizener does, that "emotional bankruptcy" is the primary cause of Dick's defeat,[9] is provocative and enlightening, but psychologically incomplete. A more probing investigation of Dick's psychological state before his marriage, especially his childhood, must be made if we are to clearly understand the basic reasons for his apparently sudden collapse. Nor is such an approach without critical precedent. Clifton Fadiman in his 1934 review of *Tender is the Night* indirectly suggested this course of interpretation when he wrote, "The actual decay of these super-civilized people . . . is traced with masterly narrative skill, but the primary causes of the decay are not clear. (Nicole's mental instability and Dick's infatuation for Rosemary are only detonators.) Dick's rapid acceptance of his failure, for instance, is not convincing; there must have been some fundamental weakness in his early youth to account for his defeatism. . . . The events of the narrative, tragic as they are, are insufficient to motivate his downfall."[10]

Fitzgerald has left behind seventeen manuscripts and a great many notes that deal with *Tender is the Night*. Presumably, in 1932 when, for the last time, he started to write the novel again, Fitzgerald made the following main outline of the story and character sketch of the hero, "The novel should do this. Show a man who is a natural idealist, a spoiled priest, giving in for various causes to the ideas of the haute Burgeoise, and in his rise to the top of the social world losing his idealism, his talent and turning to drink and dissipation. Background one in which the liesure class is at their truly most brilliant & glamorous such as Murphys."[11] The most informative but poorly understood phrase in the "Sketch" is "spoiled priest". Fitzgerald most likely borrowed the expression from James Joyce's *Ulysses* where it is applied to the young Irish romantic Stephen Daedalus. Roman Catholics generally use the phrase to describe a candidate for the priesthood who has failed to take his final vows. In the same way that one who once aspired to be a priest can retain a religious orientation and at the same time wish to take advantage of the material possibilities of the world, Dick hopes to live by his father's ideal-istic moral code and yet belong to a social class to which that code is alien. Dick, "a superman in possibilities", is the son of a Pro-testant minister from Virginia and the great-grandson of the governor of North Carolina. From his father, who came North immediately after the Civil War, Dick learned his idealism—a code of morality and a set of manners Fitzgerald always connected with the pre-Civil War South: "Dick loved his father—again and again he referred judgments to what his father would probably have thought or done. . . . He told Dick all he knew about life, not much but most of it true, simple things, matters of behavior that came within his clergyman's range. . . . His father had been sure of what he was, with a deep pride of two proud widows who had raised him to believe that nothing could be superior to 'good instincts', honor, courtesy, and courage."[12] These are the older American values of Dick's childhood that have made him "a natural idealist", "a spoiled priest", and "a moralist in revolt"[13] because he finds they have vanished from his post-World War I world. They are also the source of Dick's "tensile strength"—"the layer of hardness in him, of self-control and of self-discipline" (75)—and magnetic charm that made him "think that he wanted to be good, he wanted to be kind, he wanted to be brave and wise, but it was all pretty difficult. He wanted to be loved, too, if he could fit it in" (23). We also discover that as a child Dick watched his father's daily struggles to exist and this "wedded a desire for money to an essentially unacquisitive nature" (218). But more significant than a need for material security he believed "himself the last hope of a decaying clan". Since the Diver family has "sunk from haute burgeoisie to petit burgeoisie", Dick, like Gatsby, wanted to recover the past. Gifted with "the power of arousing a fascinating and uncritical love" (84) in people, he wanted to be all things to all men. He tried to be both a medical and spiritual doctor to Nicole, his other sick patients, and the decaying Americans around him. Dick's weaknesses and his identity as a "spoiled priest" are rooted in his personality—his egotism and desire to please and be loved that transform him into a social climber whose natural idealism is finally corrupted by the amoral values of his flock.

In Innsbruck, just before Dick hears about the lonely death of his father, the emotionally exhausted hero of *Tender is the Night* belatedly struggles toward some form of self-awareness, "He had lost himself—he could not tell the hour when, or the day or the week, the month or the year. Once he had cut through things, solving the most complicated equations as the simplest problems of his simplest patients. Between the time he found Nicole flowering under a stone on the Zürichsee and the moment of his meeting with Rosemary the spear had been blunted" (218). Dick has discovered to his horror that he no longer possesses an identity. He has lost the "tensile strength" rooted in the virtues of his father which he drew upon to perform for others what Dick calls his "trick of the heart". His formerly overflowing vitality had saved Nicole from soul-sickness and, in the manner of Jay Gatsby's parties, Dick had created a world of romantic dreams where he could bestow identities upon her and the other flawed Americans who were drawn to his promises of security. Truly "It was themselves he gave back to them, blurred by the compromises of how many years" (111). But now as an "homme epuisé" who had "wasted nine years teaching the rich the A B C's of human decency" (219), he realizes that no one can save him, not even himself. Depressed and passive he drinks heavily and is driven to irrational forms of class bigotry, particularly against Italians and Englishmen. Every attractive girl turns Dick's head although the thought of human relationships is wearisome and stale.

Personal relationships, according to Scott Fitzgerald, are at the heart of emotional bankruptcy.[14] Dick believes his marriage to Nicole—the wealthy possession of "all the lost youth in the world" (25)—and his love for Rosemary, who represented "all the immaturity of the race" (130), have drained him of his identity. Dick, however, is only partially right. His story, as James Miller maintains, is "a story of the losing of a self, the disappearance of an identity"[15] but the identity Dick once possessed was not an authentic one based upon a strongly self-delineated formation of the childhood identity elements of trust, autonomy, initiative and industry—the necessary motivation for the accomplishment of maturity. It was a pragmatic identity. Dick's growth towards maturity, the choice of psychiatry as a profession and Nicole as a wife, was not primarily the product of an interior journey but an external search that signified a retreat from the true sources of identity—the unresolved conflicts of Dick's childhood beginning with his maternal relationship.

A person achieves a true sense of identity when the *"style of one's individuality"*—one's self-image—is confirmed by "one's meaning for significant others in the immediate community".[16] This means an individual's consistent psychosocial behaviour will be clearly viewed as the essential manifestation of oneself and at the same time this communal action will be greatly supportive of the unique self one possesses and wishes to develop further. In *Tender is the Night* Fitzgerald explores the limits of Dick's pragmatic or false identity as a doctor and husband while examining his relation to a society that is fragmented and without a set of enriching values.

While Dick Diver was studying at the university a young Rumanian intellectual with whom he often argued various psychological points warned Dick about his most glaring weakness. " 'You're not a romantic philosopher—you're a scientist. Memory, force, character—especially good sense. That's going to be your trouble—judgment about yourself' " (5). After all his education at Yale, Oxford, Johns Hopkins, and Vienna, Dick remains a naïve young man lacking an adult knowledge of himself and the world. He has no idea how charming he is or that the affection he gives or inspires is really unusual. Early in the novel Fitzgerald ironically refers to his American hero as "lucky Dick" who carries with him the weaknesses and illusions of a whole nation, "Dick got up to Zurich on fewer Achilles' heels than would be required to equip a centipede, but with plenty—the illusions of eternal strength and health, and of the essential goodness of people—they were the illusions of a nation, the lies of generations of frontier mothers who had to croon falsely that there were no wolves outside the cabin door" (5).

Dick's essential nature seems to be a manifestation of what Rollo May calls "pseudoinnocence". Capitalizing on naïveté, it "consists of a childhood that is never outgrown, a kind of fixation on the past. It is childishness rather than childlikeness".[17] This pseudoinnocence blinds one to the deceptions of the self and the world. It certainly prevents Dick from fully recognizing that his original interest and commitment to psychiatry are insecurely motivated. Even before meeting Nicole Dick begins to question the high quality of his intellect. He mockingly calls his reasoning "specious" and "American—his criterion of uncerebral phrase-making was that it was American" (4–5). More significantly, Dick is uncertain

150

whether he really wants to be a psychiatrist. When studying in
Vienna his roommate Ed Elkins

> aroused in him a first faint doubt as to the quality of his mental
> processes; he could not feel that they were profoundly different
> from the thinking of Elkins—Elkins, who would name you all the
> quarterbacks at New Haven for thirty years.
>
> "—And lucky Dick can't be one of those clever men; he must
> be less intact, even faintly destroyed. If life won't do it for him
> it's not a substitute to get a disease, or a broken heart, or an
> inferiority complex, though it'd be nice to build out some broken
> side till it was better than the original structure." (4)

Erikson firmly believes that "it is the inability to settle on an
occupational identity which most disturbs young people".[18] The
choice of a profession bothers Dick, nor is the conflict short-lived.
It follows him throughout the war and back to Zurich where he
falls in love with Nicole, a rich, beautiful and very sick psychiatric
patient. Although both Franz and Dohmler clearly warn him
against marriage, advising Dick that his problem is a professional
one—an effective extension of the "transference of the most for-
tuitous kind" (9), as Franz explains it—and even Dick recognizes
the medical fact that Nicole may be a lifelong mental problem for
even the most dedicated doctor, he nevertheless marries Nicole.
Hoping to effect a cure within the marital relationship, Dick consciously retreats into the shell of a pragmatic identity and turns
his back on the unsolved conflicts of both his professional identity
and the problem of intimacy at the same time. For as A. H. Steinberg points out, "Playing doctor allows him to maintain a detached, scientific superiority which cloaks the fact that he cannot
participate as husband on an equal basis with his wife in the marriage relation".[19] What Dick really wants is a love involvement
where he is not vulnerable to the certain burdens of being emotionally involved. Dick's reactions at this crucial point in his life are
those of a child who conveniently blinds himself both to his own
ambivalent feelings and to the amoral tactics of the Warren family
who arrogantly make it very clear they are purchasing a doctor to
take care of Nicole. Dick is flirting with disaster and he knows it.
While walking with Nicole on a horseshoe walk at a mountain
resort Dick's rootless self, his reason, and the effects of years of
training all magically disappear with a kiss.

He felt the young lips, her body sighing in relief against the arm growing stronger to hold her. There were now no more plans than if Dick had arbitrarily made some undissoluble mixture, with atoms joined and inseparable; you could throw it all out but never again could they fit back into atomic scale. As he held her and tasted her, and as she curved in further and further toward him, with her own lips, new to herself, drowned and engulfed in love, yet solaced and triumphant, he was thankful to have an existence at all, if only as a reflection in her wet eyes. (47)

In the beginning of the Divers' marriage, Dick has no thought of either giving up his practice or of seeking out a life of grace and mobility which the Warren fortune can easily subsidize. But with Nicole's breakdown following the birth of their second child, Topsy, Dick allows his long-standing dissatisfaction with his profession and desires for the luxurious life of the "haute burgeoisie" to surface. Nicole has little difficulty convincing her husband that since he is bored with Zurich and has no time to write, "a confession of weakness for a scientist" (56), moving to the Riviera would be best for both of them. Nothing feeds the child in Dick more than Nicole's words, "you'll help me Dick, so I won't feel so guilty. We'll live near a warm beach where we can be brown and young together" (56). From this point on Dick registers at various lodgings as "Mr. and Mrs. Diver" rather than his usual "Doctor and Mrs. Diver". The price of Dick's intactness, his "pseudoinnocence", has now become his "incompleteness" as a psychiatrist and the gradual weakening of the pragmatic identity that has ordered his life for six years.

Since, as Dick tells Rosemary Hoyt, " 'The manner remains intact for some time after the morale cracks' " (304), the fragmented hero of *Tender is the Night* finds an outlet for his uncontrollable generosity and role playing among a small group of "nice" Americans who make the paradisiacal Riviera beach the centre of their lives of leisure and idleness. Unaware of Dick's adeptness at effortlessly manipulating the roles of doctor, lover, father, and partygiver as the occasion warrants, these expatriates find "to be included in Dick Diver's world for a while was a remarkable experience: people believed he made special reservations about them, recognizing the proud uniqueness of their destinies. He won everyone quickly with an exquisite consideration and a politeness that moved so fast and intuitively that it could be examined only in its effect. Then, without caution, lest the first bloom of the relation wither, he opened the gate to his amusing world" (84). Dick has the genius for creating a life of enchanting beauty for Nicole and their friends. We are shown his success by Rosemary's uncritical admiration for this breathtaking existence which she soon realizes depends solely upon Dick's vitality and grace. Yet Dick's interest in the group around him is not entirely selfless. He needs their love and approval to appease his desires to be accepted as a member of the "haute burgeoisie". Moreover, since Dick has lost his capacity for work and is no longer Dr. Diver they also supply him in part with a pragmatic identity.

Erikson characterizes ego-identity as "the actually attained but forever to-be-revised sense of reality of the Self within social reality. . . . One can then speak of ego identity when one discusses the ego's synthesizing power in the light of its central psycho-social function, and of self-identity when the integration of the individual's self- and role-images are under discussion."[20] Dick's roles as a doctor-husband to Nicole and spiritual father to a group of rich expatriates represent his achievement of ego-identity. Yet he is not satisfied with these accomplishments. Deep within his consciousness Dick constantly opposes to this pragmatic ego-identity his own notion of the Self rooted in the traditional virtues of his father, "honor, courtesy, and courage". As Arthur Mizener points out so well, "In Dick's best moment, *Tender is the Night* shows us how beautiful the realized ideal life is; but in the end it shows us that people with the sensitivity and imagination to conceive that life cannot survive among the rich."[21]

Dick likewise cannot function within a society whose characters are similar to those in Eliot's *The Waste Land*, a society that has abandoned its former values and now believes, as Mary North says, " 'All people want is to have a good time and if you make them unhappy you cut yourself off from nourishment' " (332). A world inhabited by Nicole and Baby Warren, Abe North, the McKiscos, Tommy Barban and their life is more of a menace than a refuge for Dick. It apparently fulfils his need for an identity based upon an insatiable thirst for affection and a sense of belonging to the "furthermost evolution of a class". Still Dick finds that his activity within this society is not truly enhancing of the self he uniquely is but also wishes to hide. Only Nicole senses something of the price Dick is paying for living too long with a self-image that is not confirmed by society.

> He went back into his house and Nicole saw that one of his most characteristic moods was upon him, the excitement that swept everyone up into it and was inevitably followed by his own form of melancholy, which he never displayed but at which she guessed. This excitement about things reached an intensity out of proportion to their importance, generating a really extraordinary virtuosity with people. Save among a few of the tough-minded and perennially suspicious, he had the power of arousing a fascinating and uncritical love. The reaction came when he realized the waste and extravagance involved. He sometimes looked back with awe at the carnivals of affection he had given, as a general might gaze upon a massacre he had ordered to satisfy an impersonal blood lust. (84)

These periods of melancholy, a major symptom of Dick's decreasing vitality, occur more frequently. Although he is well aware of the quality of the various people feeding upon him, Dick cannot detach himself from them until it is too late. He is like an adolescent desperately in search of his true identity who attempts to arrive at a definition of his identity by projecting his diffused self-image on another and by seeing it thus reflected and gradually clarified. Dick, however, as he looks about him, sees characters who, as James Miller says, "reflect one or another of his weaknesses in isolation. . . . Money, Liquor, Anarchy, Self-Betrayal, Sex. These abstractions take carnal embodiment in Baby Warren, Abe North, Tommy Barban, Albert McKisco, and Rosemary Hoyt."[22] Dick's need to cater to these neurotics is his fatal wound, a "lesion of vitality" in Fitzgerald's words, which finally drains him of his energy.

Another more obvious consequence of Dick's loss of a pragmatic identity with its quota of vitality is his inability to control himself. The earliest signs of this change occur when he meets Rosemary Hoyt on the beach at Antibes. Since Nicole has slowly begun to recover from her illness and is no longer completely dependent upon him, Dick finds Rosemary very attractive. Within a few days he tells her " 'You're the only girl I've seen for a long time that actually did look like something blooming' " (77). Like the teenage Nicole, Rosemary is portrayed as being childishly seductive.

Her "cheeks lit to a lovely flame, like the thrilling flush of children after their cold baths in the evening. . . . Her body hovered delicately on the last edge of childhood—she was almost eighteen, nearly complete, but the dew was still on her" (58–9). Dick at thirty-four is almost twice Rosemary's age. He is well aware of this fact as well as her immature tendency to idolize him and her mother. Yet for all her inexperience Rosemary senses the shallowness of Dick's relationship with Nicole. She compares it to the love of herself and her mother and questions "When people have so much for outsiders didn't it indicate a lack of inner intensity?" (137).

Although Dick falls in love with Rosemary, he refuses her offer of an affair on the grounds that he is "old fashioned". Dick wants Rosemary to meet her first lover "all intact" (127). He also fears the knowledge of such a relationship would hurt Nicole whom he still claims to love. Yet even this apparently ethical act of refusal leaves its psychological mark upon Dick; "for a moment his usual grace, the tensile strength of his balance, was absent" (127). It cannot wipe away the fact that Dick has consciously allowed himself to drift into an obviously neurotic relationship; he tells Rosemary, " 'When a child can disturb a middle-aged gent—things get difficult' " (154). For Dick the most shattering aspect of the experience is the growing awareness that he is deeply vulnerable. An impressionable starlet, exuding the "persistent aroma of the nursery" (179), had broken through his defences and entered that part of Dick's mind where he had buried his fundamental self amid "the tawdry souvenirs of his boyhood" (212). Such penetration means he can no longer rely upon the shell of his pragmatic identity as doctor-husband to Nicole and "spoiled priest" of the rich to prevent his descent to a particular phase of psychological malignancy Erikson calls "the rock-bottom attitude". This consists of an individual's almost deliberate surrender to the pull of a radical search for the ultimate limit of his own personal regression.[23]

The assumption of such a search may be manifested in "an impulsive flight into sexual promiscuity acted out without sexual satisfaction or any sense of participation; enormously absorbing rituals of masturbation or food intake; excessive drinking or wild driving; or self-destructive marathons of reading or listening to music without thought of food or sleep".[24] At the same time Erikson believes that at the centre of such negative activities the individual may discover the need "to redelineate himself" and therefore begin to rebuild the foundation of his authentic identity, the only firm foundation for healthy human development. In this way what may seem to be the onset of neurosis often is an aggravated crisis which might prove self-liquidating and contribute to the process of authentic identity formation.

Dick's affair with Rosemary is the turning point in his psychological life, his surrender to "the rock-bottom attitude". Possessing such a vast store of unresolved childhood conflicts he has been drawn to an "infant", as he calls her, who has become "a symbol of remembrance" recalling him to his youth, the ultimate cause of his false and unhappy present life.[25] Although Rosemary leaves and Dick tries to pass off his infatuation for her as a comfortable interlude in his life, the amorphous process of regression continues. He finds himself drinking a little too much. Relations with Nicole and other adults become strained. His research and clinical work have long lost their appeal. Like an awkward adolescent Dick begins to focus upon the "unripened youth" of women. At St. Moritz when Nicole suggests he dance with a teenage girl, he refuses saying " 'When I dance with them, I feel as if I'm pushing a baby carriage' " (188). His interest in his own children borders on the unnatural. Dick feels there is no essential difference between his infant daughter and Rosemary, both are "young and magnetic".

While Dick continues his descent to "rock-bottom", Nicole rises amid occasional setbacks to new levels of stability and self-discovery. With health and independence comes the awareness that "She hated the beach, resented the places where she had played planet to Dick's sun" (307). As expected, her true Warren self emerges and she turns to a new lover, Tommy Barban, who is quick to see the change in her eyes. He asks Nicole " 'When did you begin to have white crook's eyes?' " She replies " '. . . it's because I'm well again. And being well perhaps I've gone back to my true self—I suppose my grandfather was a crook and I'm a crook by heritage, so there we are' " (310–11).

Shortly after the death of his father Dick makes one last attempt to salvage his years of emotional investment in the world of the "haute burgeoisie". He takes a three months leave of absence from the clinic in order to rest and think. While in Rome he meets

Rosemary and hoping for some magical transformation consummates their love affair which had begun four years earlier. The encounter reveals there is little true love in their relationship. Dick hoped to find a renewal of life but he found only a "black death", feeling like a man who had "raped a five-year-old girl". Yet such guilt suggests that Dick finally recognizes the severity of his neurosis—his lack of an authentic identity and the basic inability to love and allow himself to be loved that no professional success or personal charm could ultimately fill.

"True 'engagement' with others is the result and the test of firm self-delineation."[26] One cannot fail to notice how Dick Diver, a psychiatrist, is singularly unable to make use of this traditional principle of human development in his own life. Even at the end of *Tender is the Night*, in an obvious state of complete emotional exhaustion, Dick still tries to justify his adult life of self-destructive relationships by projecting his inadequacy upon Nicole. Twelve years, however, have brought about a reversal of roles. Nicole is now in possession of their one identity; she is the doctor but, unlike Dick, is capable of treating a self-pitying patient with the words of objective truth. " 'You're a coward! You've made a failure of your life, and want to blame it on me' " (319). The power of Nicole's words breaks through the brittle remains of Dick's defences. After Nicole leaves "he leaned his head forward on the parapet. The case was finished, Doctor Diver was at liberty" (320), a tragic truth it has taken him so long to realize.

Dick Diver has finally reached his "rock-bottom attitude". He is now free to "redelineate" himself and begin again his search for an authentic identity based upon a true knowledge of self and others. But now it seems to be too late for Dick; he has been drawing too long upon emotional resources he does not possess. He has become, as Fitzgerald writes in "The Crack-Up", "like a little boy left alone in a big house, who knew that now he could do anything he wanted to do, but found that there was nothing that he wanted to do".[27] Dick decides to return to America and open an office in Buffalo, New York, where his minister father died, the man from whom he inherited the belief that "nothing could be superior to 'good instincts', honor, courtesy, and courage" (221). The day of his departure Diver lingers on the beach much to the displeasure of Baby Warren who finds his lack of "delicacy" offensive. Although Nicole comes to Dick's defence, her sister coldly but wisely summarizes Dick's chief weakness. "'When people are taken out of their depths they lose their heads, no matter how charming a bluff they put up'" (331).

Although Baby Warren is one of the minor figures in *Tender is the Night*, a knowledge of the source and function of her character is essential if we are to understand why Dick turned his back upon his true self and assumed the pragmatic identity of a doctor-husband within a glittering, but empty, society, an act that ultimately brought about his downfall. On the most obvious level Baby Warren represents the impersonal power of wealth. Although she is socially and emotionally immature, "there was something wooden and onanistic about her" (44). Baby epitomizes both the sterility of a life dedicated to money and the poisonous influence such an amoral person can wield among wiser and apparently humane people. In *Tender is the Night*, as James Miller points out, "she plays the role of evil genius, mysteriously materializing at all the crucial moments of [Dick's] life and subtly dictating his every important decision".[28] Her scheme "to buy Nicole a doctor", brings about Dick and Nicole's marriage. She supplies the Warren money so Dick may become a partner in a psychiatric clinic. Baby's influence frees Dick from prison in Rome. There is little evidence in the novel that she ever falls under the spell of Dick's charm. In fact, if, as Dick believes, "he had been swallowed up like a gigolo and had somehow permitted his arsenal to be locked up in the Warren safety-deposit vault" (218–19), Baby Warren was the chief architect of the plan and never relinquished the keys.

Yet Baby Warren could not have been so successful unless she had found a deep responding chord in her victim. "Lucky Dick" had the talent to evoke uncritical love in people, especially women, and control them with its power. But, as Richard Lehan explains, his contact with women, Nicole and Rosemary in particular, tends to function best within a father-daughter relationship.[29] When this protective control weakens or disappears, Dick is unable to raise himself to a higher level of maturity where he could experience adult love and sexuality. Only Baby Warren from the very beginning senses this fundamental character flaw in Dick and uses it to her complete advantage. Her method is to treat him as a calculating or neurotic mother might deal with a son whose life she is determined to dominate. Dick Diver makes only two passing

references to his own mother in *Tender is the Night* but his behaviour is that of a young boy who has not grown up and is still
under the psychological control of a dominant mother or is impotent in the presence of the strongly maternal Baby Warren. Dick
said he lost himself during the interval between finding Nicole and
meeting Rosemary. What he lost, as stated earlier, was merely a
pragmatic identity.

His chances for the achievement of an authentic identity and
maturity were lost or greatly diminished years before when death
struck his family shortly before his birth. In *Tender is the Night*,
the author writes, "Dick was born several months after the death
of two young sisters and his father, guessing what would be the
effect on Dick's mother, had saved him from a spoiling by becoming his moral guide. He was tired stock yet he raised himself
to that effort" (221). Shortly afterward Fitzgerald adds, "The
father always considered that his wife's small fortune belonged to
his son, and in college and in medical school sent him a check
for all the income four times a year" (221). Only one other reference is made to Dick's mother in the novel and this is indirect, the
fact that the father had survived his wife. Most critics of Fitzgerald agree with Henry Dan Piper that the author turned to the
image and memory of his own father, Edward Fitzgerald, when he
created the character of Dick's father. He represents the moral
touchstone, "the good instincts—honor, courtesy, courage", to
which the hero continually returns until exhaustion and apathy
firmly take hold.[30] But the few lines Fitzgerald devoted to
Dick's mother and the history of the mother figure during the
author's long struggle to complete *Tender is the Night* perhaps
supply a more probable reason for Dick's much criticized downfall.

Fitzgerald, like Dick Diver, was born shortly after the death of
two sisters but his father, unlike Dick's father, had not saved him
from a spoiling by the mother, the effect of which was Fitzgerald's
failure as an infant to establish a basic sense of trust, the foundation of an authentic identity. This inadequacy, as we have seen,
dictated the style of his development through the subsequent
stages of life, especially the pivotal crisis of identity. An examination of Fitzgerald's early attempts to write more fully and explicitly about the mother of the projected hero of *Tender is the
Night* as well as the major traits of orality in Dick Diver's char-

acter raise serious doubts whether Dick's father truly saved his son from a mother's spoiling and the fundamental weaknesses of such a relationship.

Matthew Bruccoli in his book on the composition of *Tender is the Night* has shown that Fitzgerald spent four years, 1925–1929, trying to develop a novel based upon a matricide plot.[31] The concrete result of this effort was a story of twenty thousand words which Fitzgerald considered calling "The Boy Who Killed His Mother". It deals with the experiences of a successful and talented Hollywood movie technician, Francis Melarky, during a vacation on the Riviera with his mother Charlotte. The father is in prison serving a long sentence for some violent crime. There are suggestions that Francis has inherited his father's quick and fiery temper. The mother is strongly possessive and domineering. Her attempts to control Francis have long since created bad feelings between them. Yet she is persistent in her demands and frequently excites her son by reminding him of his past failures. No plot summary has survived for the account of the matricide. Most likely Fitzgerald never prepared one. Yet it is quite clear Fitzgerald intended to have Francis kill his mother later in the book. In 1926 he requested legal information from Maxwell Perkins. "Will you ask somebody what is done if one American murders another in France."[32]

In examining Fitzgerald's motivation for the selection of a matricide plot, one must bear in mind the author's own experiences and ambivalent feelings about his mother. There seems to be little doubt that in some major ways she served as a model for the domineering Charlotte Melarky, Francis' mother. Another source was Walker Ellis, an American expatriate Fitzgerald originally met at Princeton where he was an object of the author's adolescent hero worship. Ellis was on the Riviera when Fitzgerald was and became a model for Francis Melarky. Gerald Murphy recalls that Ellis "was much on Scott's mind. He spoke often of him to me."[33]

Fitzgerald eventually found the story of Francis Melarky and matricide too difficult to handle. In 1929 he abandoned the general project in favour of a "new angle". Yet, as Bruccoli maintains, "the gestation of the Dick Diver version is readily seen during this period".[34] Fitzgerald salvaged much of the Melarky material for later use in *Tender is the Night*—his experiences with two homosexuals on the beach, the hero being mistaken for a rapist by a crowd outside the court, and most importantly, his drunken brawl with some cab drivers in Rome. Badly beaten by the police Francis is rescued by his mother who, like Baby Warren in *Tender is the Night*, has sought aid at the American Embassy and Consulate. This last fact is but one piece of evidence supporting the claims of Bruccoli[35] and Lehan[36] that the spirit of Baby Warren's character developed in Fitzgerald's mind out of his original conception of Charlotte Melarky. Although Fitzgerald once again failed to confront and explicitly expose the influence of the mother on his hero's development and downfall in *Tender is the Night*, it is present, although disguised, in the character of Baby Warren. She has the same kind of intuitive knowledge of Dick that a mother has for her child, and she is the only one who is never blinded by Dick's pragmatic identity and is therefore able to exploit his basic immaturity. For Baby Warren Dick was always a doctor, and his relationship with Nicole, as she tells her sister on the day he leaves, was "what he was educated for" (331).

This is the voice of the amoral rich speaking, but Dick is not a tragic victim. He played into their hands because of his insatiable oral need to be needed and loved. This desire remained with him to the very end. His last conversation with Mary North, whose first husband Abe was an alcoholic, highlights Dick's downfall and the oral symptoms it manifests.

> "Your friends still like you, Dick. But you say awful things to people when you've been drinking. I've spent most of my time defending you this summer."
>
> "That remark is one of Doctor Eliot's classics."
>
> "It's true. Nobody cares whether you drink or not—" She hesitated, "Even when Abe drank hardest, he never offended people like you do. . . ."
>
> Dick felt fine—he was already well in advance of the day, arrived at where a man should be at the end of a good dinner, yet he showed only a fine, considered restrained interest in Mary. His eyes, for the moment clear as a child's, asked her sympathy and stealing over him he felt the old necessity of convincing her that he was the last man in the world and she was the last woman. . . .
>
> "You once liked me, didn't you?" he asked.
>
> "*Liked* you—I *loved* you. Everybody loved you. You could've had anybody you wanted for the asking——" (332)

Images of orality, which constantly surround Fitzgerald's depiction of his hero, reach their highest level in this final picture of him as a helpless child pleading for nourishment. The ultimate cause of Dick's pitiful condition is not "a sinister kind of innocence" or "emotional bankruptcy", but the fact that Dick's authentic identity formation never began with the first true meeting of mother and child.

Although Fitzgerald does not evoke Dick's childhood, we can derive Dick's defective resolution of the primary crisis of childhood—the crisis of basic trust—from his various forms of compulsive orality, the most notable of these, as we have seen, being his drinking and insatiable need for love. There are others. Dick, like Anthony Patch, feels a "nostalgia for a lost paradise" which he believes the "haute burgeoisie" world of the very rich will appease. Fitzgerald also portrays Dick's facility with words as one of the effects of Dick's seductive charm. "His voice, with some faint Irish melody running through it, wooed the world. . . .[It] promised that he would take care of her, and that a little later he would open up whole new worlds for her, unroll an endless succession of magnificent possibilities" (72).

Throughout *Tender is the Night* in one confrontation after another, occupational, social, sexual, Dick reveals a fundamental pattern of oral incorporation. This form of intercourse with the world suggests the dimensions of the psychological problem Dick confronts as a developing self deprived of its infantile foundation of basic trust. Although he has used this pathology creatively for a time—he worked extremely hard to become a psychiatrist and to charm his friends—Dick's progression through the early stages of development have been insecurely motivated because of a lack of trust. Behind his pragmatic identity, which allows him to evoke love, is a blindness to his dissipation of his talents as a doctor and a man among people who give him little true fulfilment in return. But Dick is not and perhaps never will be ready to give up this protective form of behaviour no matter what happens. His fear of adult responsibility and love is too strong and deeply-seated.

Dick's behaviour, especially after he meets Nicole and Rosemary, becomes more and more regressive and childish. His failure to progress through the stages of psychosocial development has left him with a fixation upon the primary stage of orality. Dick has apparently passed through the painful years of adolescence with a certain ease. But beneath his charm and generosity remains an insecure self clinging to his childhood pattern of oral behaviour. This apparently was his chief protection against a dominating, overaffectionate mother. In addition Dick's adult behaviour reveals an identification with a controlling mother figure. He is easily drawn into relationships where others are clearly submissive or generally dependent upon him.

This pathology, however, ultimately becomes more virulent and self-destructive. Oftentimes, as Otto Fenichel writes, "the adult person gets into situations in which he is again as helpless as he was as a child; sometimes forces of nature are responsible, but more often social forces created by men".[37] Dick Diver reaches the ultimate limit of regression within his "rock-bottom attitude" when Nicole turns instinctively from him towards Barban and he finds himself totally alone and emotionally exhausted. Soon after "the old interior laughter had begun inside him and he knew he couldn't keep it up much longer" (333). Dick Diver's attempts to avoid a true identity through the assumption of a pragmatic identity have finally brought him to the depths of a stage of psychological malignancy. Although this condition may often become the firm foundation for self-redelineation and a renewed progression towards an authentic identity, Dick Diver, as Fitzgerald would have us believe at the end of *Tender is the Night*, apparently did not have the vitality he needed to prepare for the second act of his life. But Dick's deficiency is not unexpected. For too long he had been only a mediocre caretaker of himself.

Dick Diver fails as all the other previous heroes of Fitzgerald's completed novels fail. He manifests a lack of solidity in his identity as did the others. But Dick Diver is the one we would least expect to have failed. He possessed so many superior character traits, his ability to evoke uncritical love, intelligence, charm, and the advantages of a strong moral heritage from his father and long years of study at prominent schools, all of which we conventionally consider the signs of stability and success.

Throughout his novels Fitzgerald has been upping the psychological ante on each of his main characters. He begins with an immature adolescent, Amory Blaine, and shows his weaknesses. In *The Beautiful and Damned* Anthony Patch betrays his idealistic longings and loses his youth and sanity in his quest for money. Fitzgerald continues with the energetic Gatsby who also is roman-

163

tic and critically weak. He climaxes with the very respectable, learned doctor, researcher, and writer, Dick Diver, and finds him also essentially wanting. There is little doubt that Fitzgerald, like Erikson, sees the problem of identity as extremely crucial yet equally complex.

NOTES

1 Turnbull, p. 241.
2 Fitzgerald, *Letters*, p. 388.
3 Fitzgerald, *Letters*, p. 388–9.
4 Malcolm Cowley, *Three Novels of F. Scott Fitzgerald* (New York: Scribner's, 1953), p. vi.
5 Matthew J. Bruccoli, *The Composition of Tender is the Night: A Study of the Manuscripts* (Pittsburgh: University of Pittsburgh Press, 1963), pp. 5–12.
6 Fitzgerald, *Letters*, p. 590.
7 Miller, p. 141.
8 Miller, p. 141.
9 Mizener, pp. 270–1.
10 Bruccoli, p. 6.
11 Mizener, pp. 345–6.
12 F. Scott Fitzgerald, *Tender is the Night*, in *Three Novels of F. Scott Fitzgerald*, ed. Malcolm Cowley (New York: Scribner's, 1955), pp. 220–1. All further quotations are from this edition; page reference will be indicated after the quotation.
13 Mizener, p. 345–6.
14 Fitzgerald, "The Crack-Up", p. 69–84.
15 Miller, p. 140.
16 Erikson, *Identity*, p. 50.
17 Rollo May, *Power and Innocence: A Search for the Sources of Violence* (New York: Norton, 1972), p. 49.
18 Erikson, *Identity*, p. 132.
19 Abraham H. Steinberg, "Fitzgerald's Portrait of a Psychiatrist", in *Tender is the Night: Essays in Criticism*, ed. Marvin J. LaHood (Bloomington, Ind.: Indiana University Press, 1969), p. 141.
20 Erikson, *Identity*, p. 211.
21 Arthur M. Mizener, "Tender is the Night", in *Tender is the Night: Essays in Criticism*, p. 108.
22 Miller, pp. 142–3.
23 Erikson, *Identity*, p. 212–13.
24 Erikson, *Identity*, p. 214.
25 Sklar, p. 276.
26 Erikson, *Identity*, p. 167.
27 Fitzgerald, "The Crack-Up", p. 79.

28 Miller, p. 143.
29 Lehan, p. 135.
30 Piper, p. 12.
31 Bruccoli, pp. 17–58.
32 Fitzgerald, *Dear Scott/Dear Max*, p. 120.
33 Bruccoli, pp. 21–2.
34 Bruccoli, p. 58.
35 Bruccoli, pp. 28–31.
36 Lehan, p. 129.
37 Fenichel, p. 492.

Epilogue

Erik Erikson's psychoanalytic theories, rooted in the belief that personal growth and communal culture are inseparable, have seemed to offer a uniquely appropriate means for examining the American identity crisis of Scott Fitzgerald and those of the major male characters in his four completed novels. *American* here implies a naïve but not deterministic belief in the limitless material promises of American life and the rejection of all forms of deprivation in view of the limitless resources the land seemed to offer. But inherent in this romantic American vision of life is a critical deficiency, an anti-historical bias that hoped to live unaffected by the scales of traditional values that have ordered life in other societies.

Fitzgerald's life, especially his complex relationship with his wife, Zelda, both exemplifies and exposes the limitations of this kind of social faith. It has been the ground, therefore, of this study both because Fitzgerald is himself the example and because the subject of his best writing was always his own "transmuted biography". From the time of Fitzgerald's teenage *Thoughtbook* until he died desperately trying to complete *The Last Tycoon*, he wrote almost exclusively about his own tormented self and Zelda. Their relationship from the start was hardly a romantic fable. They shared not only beauty, vitality, and ambition; they likewise shared deep feelings of inferiority and conflict about their identities that ironically contributed to their lifelong loyalty to one another.

Unfortunately this likeness was the source of self-destructive tendencies in Scott and of a feeling of jealous rivalry in Zelda. When the Fitzgeralds married in 1920, Scott was well aware of the essential part Zelda played in his identity as a man and a writer. He viewed the two of them as one person and Zelda's life as his exclusive property. Zelda initially believed that she wanted this kind of dependent identity. Soon, however, she grew resentful and sought to be independent of her husband's influence. But the price of this venture was an interior conflict about her identity as a woman who wanted both to pursue her true self and still to be protected. The conflict resulted in her psychological collapse and confinement in a mental hospital.

The Fitzgeralds' subsequent life was very much a struggle for survival. Scott dedicated himself to reconstructing his relationship with an often hostile Zelda. He could not give her up, nor could he stop drinking or forgive himself for his part in her illness. A different kind of mutual attachment developed, "less a romance than a categorical imperative", as Scott described it, which contained strong elements of love and courage. But to call the Fitzgeralds' marriage a failure, as some biographers have, is myopic. It overlooks the painful, often mysterious, complexities of intimacy in the search for identity.

Unlike Scott Fitzgerald, the heroes of his completed novels almost entirely fail in their individual pursuits of identity, love, and maturity. In each case their psychological backgrounds have left them ill-equipped to succeed at work and intimacy. They are all men who long to be socially recognized and loved. But they seem to desire failure and self-destruction more. In the professional or business world the Fitzgerald hero finds little fulfilment. Amory Blaine never commits himself to any profession. Anthony Patch avoids work if possible and childishly but firmly waits for his rich grandfather's death that will make him financially independent and safe for life. Although Dick Diver works hard to become a promising psychiatrist, he ends up as a doctor incapable of functioning as a general practitioner. The single apparent success is Jay Gatsby; yet his riches are accumulated through dubious means and cannot purchase Daisy.

In the pursuit of his identity through heterosexual intimacy the Fitzgerald hero experiences the same failure. Each searches out a woman who will leave him rejected, emasculated, or even dead. Rosalind, after a brief passionate affair with Amory that includes plans for marriage, rejects him for the security of the millionaire Dawson Ryder. Gloria Gilbert marries Anthony yet their union proves fatal because Gloria's selfish aggressiveness is partially responsible for her husband's depression, alcoholism, and insanity. At the end of the novel, the marriage remains but only Gloria can enjoy the money. Daisy openly proclaims her love for Gatsby before Tom. Hours later, however, she leaves town with her husband knowing that Gatsby will have to bear the responsibility for her crime of killing Myrtle. In *Tender is the Night* Franz warns Dick Diver against his plan of trying to cure Nicole through a marital relationship. Dick disregards this advice and cures his patient-wife, who then deserts him in favour of the stronger Tommy Barban. Nicole's return to health and subsequent rejection drains Dick of almost all the vitality or hope he posssesses.

Fitzgerald roots these various failures both in the weaknesses of the individuals and in a more fundamental weakness in the American belief in unlimited possibility. In contrast, Fitzgerald tried to order his life according to the more traditional norms of "honor, courtesy, and courage". Right up to the evening he died, 20 December 1940, he was courageously trying to complete *The Last Tycoon*. The fact is significant. For years Scott had felt that he spoke and acted only with the authority of failure. Hopefully this study has helped to throw a more forgiving or understanding light on his own sense of failure. Time, as well as his determined work to the end, has certainly indicated that beyond his sense of personal failure lies the figure of a successful man whose life and writings have left a distinctive mark upon American literature. Fitzgerald's personal failures taught him to make successful fictional images of basic psychological drives with which all of us contend.

Selected Bibliography

Allen, Frederick L., *Only Yesterday* (New York: Bantam, 1959)

Arieti, Silvano, M.D., *Interpretation of Schizophrenia* (New York: Basic Books, 1974)

Bewley, Marius, "Great Scott", *New York Review of Books*, 16 September 1965, p. 23

—— *The Eccentric Design: Form in the Classic American Novel* (New York: Columbia University Press, 1963)

Boyd, Ernest, *Portraits: Real and Imaginary* (London: Jonathan Cape, 1924)

Bruccoli, Matthew J., *The Composition of Tender is the Night: A Study of the Manuscripts* (Pittsburgh: University of Pittsburgh Press, 1963)

—— ed., *Fitzgerald/Hemingway Annual* (Washington, D.C.: Microcard Editions, 1969–75)

—— *Fitzgerald Newsletter* (Washington, D.C., Microcard Editions, 1969)

Bryer, Jackson, *The Critical Reputation of F. Scott Fitzgerald: A Bibliographical Study* (Hamden, Conn.: Shoestring Press, 1967)

—— ed., *Sixteen Modern American Authors* (New York: Norton, 1973)

Burbans, Clinton S., Jr., "Structure and Theme in *This Side of Paradise*", *Journal of English and Germanic Philology*, 68 (1969), 604–24

Callahan, John F., *The Illusions of a Nation: Myth and History in the Novels of F. Scott Fitzgerald* (Urbana, Ill.: University of Illinois Press, 1972)

Coles, Robert, *Erik H. Erikson: The Growth of His Work* (Boston: Atlantic-Little, Brown, 1970)

—— "Shrinking History–Part I", *New York Review of Books*, 22 February 1973, pp. 15–21

—— "Shrinking History–Part II", *New York Review of Books*, 8 March 1973, pp. 25–9

Commager, Henry Steele, *The American Mind* (New Haven: Yale University Press, 1950)

Cowley, Malcolm, "Fitzgerald: The Double Man", *Saturday Review*, 24 February 1951, pp. 9–10, 42–4

Cowley, Malcolm, "Introduction", in *Three Novels of F. Scott Fitzgerald*, ed. Malcolm Cowley and Edmund Wilson (New York: Scribner's, 1953)

Eble, Kenneth E., *F. Scott Fitzgerald* (New York: Twayne, 1977)

Elkind, David, "Erik Erikson's Eight Ages of Man", *New York Times Magazine Section*, 5 April 1970, 25–7, 84–92, 110–19

Erikson, Erik H., *Childhood and Society* (New York: Norton, 1963)

—— *Dimensions of a New Identity* (New York: Norton, 1974)

—— *Gandhi's Truth: On the Origins of Militant Nonviolence* (New York: Norton, 1969)

—— *Identity: Youth and Crisis* (New York: Norton, 1968)

—— *Insight and Responsibility* (New York: Norton, 1964)

—— *Life History and the Historical Moment* (New York: Norton, 1975)

—— "The Roots of Virtue", in *The Humanist Frame*, ed. J. Huxley (New York: Harper and Row, 1961) pp. 145–66

—— *Young Man Luther: A Study in Psychoanalysis and History* (New York: Norton, 1958)

Evans, Richard I., *Dialogue with Erikson* (New York: Dutton, 1969)

Fenichel, Otto, *The Psychoanalytic Theory of Neurosis* (New York: Norton, 1945)

Fitzgerald, F. Scott, *Afternoon of an Author: A Selection of Uncollected Stories and Essays*, ed. Arthur M. Mizener (New York: Scribner's, 1957)

—— *Babylon Revisited and Other Stories* (New York: Scribner's, 1960)

—— *Dear Scott/Dear Max*, ed. John Kuehl and Jackson Bryer (New York: Scribner's, 1971)

—— *Tender is the Night*, ed. Malcolm Cowley, *Three Novels of F. Scott Fitzgerald* (New York: Scribner's, 1953)

—— *The Apprentice Fiction of F. Scott Fitzgerald, 1909–1917*, ed. John Kuehl (New Brunswick: Rutgers University Press, 1965)

—— *The Beautiful and Damned* (New York: Scribner's, 1922)

—— *The Crack-Up*, ed. Edmund Wilson (New York: New Directions, 1945)

—— *The Last Tycoon*, ed. Edmund Wilson, *Three Novels of F. Scott Fitzgerald* (New York: Scribner's, 1953)

—— *The Letters of F. Scott Fitzgerald*, ed. Andrew Turnbull (New York: Scribner's, 1963)

—— *The Great Gatsby* (New York: Scribner's, 1925)

—— *The Stories of F. Scott Fitzgerald*, ed. Malcolm Cowley (New York: Scribner's, 1951)

—— *This Side of Paradise* (New York: Scribner's, 1920)

170

Fitzgerald, Zelda, *Save Me the Waltz* (Carbondale: Southern Illinois University Press, 1967)

Freud, Sigmund, *Leonardo da Vinci and a Memory of His Childhood* (New York: Norton, 1964)

—— *The Basic Writings of Sigmund Freud* (New York: *Modern Library*, 1938)

Fussel, Edwin, "Fitzgerald's Brave New World", in *F. Scott Fitzgerald: A Collection of Critical Essays*, ed. Arthur M. Mizener (Englewood Cliffs, N.J.: Prentice-Hall, 1963) pp. 43–56

Goldhurst, William, *F. Scott Fitzgerald and His Contemporaries* (Cleveland: World, 1963)

Hall, C. and G. Lindzey, *Theories of Personality* (New York: Wiley, 1970)

Heath, Mary, "Marriages: Scott and Zelda, Eleanor and Franklin", *The Massachusetts Review*, 13 (Winter/Spring 1972), 281–88

Higgins, John A., *F. Scott Fitzgerald: A Study of the Stories* (New York: St. John's University Press, 1971)

Hoffman, Frederick J., *Freudianism and the Literary Mind* (Baton Rouge: Louisiana State University Press, 1957)

—— *The Twenties* (New York: Collier, 1955)

—— ed., *The Great Gatsby: A Study* (New York: Scribner's, 1962)

Horney, Karen, *The Collected Works of Karen Horney*, I (New York: Norton, 1963)

Janeway, Elizabeth, "*Zelda: A Biography*", *Saturday Review*, 13 June 1970, p. 30

Kahn, Sy, "*This Side of Paradise:* The Pageantry of Disillusion", *The Midwest Quarterly*, 7 (1966), 177–94

Kazin, Alfred, ed., *F. Scott Fitzgerald: The Man and His Work* (New York: World, 1951)

LaHood, Marvin, J., ed., *Tender is the Night: Essays in Criticism* (Bloomington: Indiana University Press, 1969)

Latham, Aaron, *Crazy Sundays: F. Scott Fitzgerald in Hollywood* (New York: Viking, 1970)

Lehan, Richard D., *F. Scott Fitzgerald and the Craft of Fiction* (Carbondale: Southern Illinois University Press, 1966)

Leuchtenburg, William E., *The Perils of Prosperity, 1914–32* (Chicago: University of Chicago Press, 1958)

Lindzey, Gardner, ed., *Handbook of Social Psychology* (Cambridge: Addison-Wesley, 1954)

Lockridge, Ernest, ed., *Twentieth Century Interpretations of The Great Gatsby* (Englewood Cliffs, N.J.: Prentice-Hall, 1968)

Maier, Henry W., *Three Theories of Child Development* (New York: Harper and Row, 1969)

171

May, Rollo, *Power and Innocence: A Search for the Sources of Violence* (New York: Norton, 1972)

Mencken, H. L., "Books More or Less Amusing", *The Smart Set*, 62 (September 1920), 140

Milford, Nancy, *Zelda: A Biography* (New York: Harper and Row, 1970)

Miller, James E., *F. Scott Fitzgerald: His Art and His Technique* (New York: New York University Press, 1964)

Mizener, Arthur M., "Tender is the Night" in *Tender is the Night: Essays in Criticism*, ed. Marvin J. LaHood (Bloomington: Indiana University Press, 1969) pp. 107–17

—— *The Far Side of Paradise: A Critical Biography of F. Scott Fitzgerald* (Boston: Houghton Mifflin, 1965)

—— ed., *F. Scott Fitzgerald: A Collection of Critical Essays* (Englewood Cliffs, N.J.: Prentice-Hall, 1963)

Mok, Michel, "A Writer Like Me Must Have an Utter Confidence, an Utter Faith in His Star", in *F. Scott Fitzgerald In His Own Times: A Miscellany*, ed. Matthew Bruccoli and Jackson Bryer (Kent, Ohio: Kent State University Press, 1971) pp. 294–99

Monroe, Ruth L., *Schools of Psychoanalytic Thought: An Exposition, Critique and Attempt at Integration* (New York: Holt, Rinehart and Winston, 1955)

Perosa, Sergio, *The Art of F. Scott Fitzgerald*, trans. Charles Matz and Sergio Perosa (Ann Arbor: University of Michigan Press, 1965)

Piper, Henry D., *F. Scott Fitzgerald: A Critical Portrait* (New York: Holt, Rinehart and Winston, 1965)

Roazen, Paul, *Erik H. Erikson: The Power and Limits of a Vision* (New York: Free Press, 1976)

Rose, Ellen C., "Doris Lessing's *Children of Violence* as a Bildungsroman: An Eriksonian Analysis", unpublished Ph.D. dissertation, University of Masschusetts, 1974

Rosenfeld, Paul, "Fitzgerald before *The Great Gatsby*", in *F. Scott Fitzgerald: The Man and His Work*, ed. Alfred Kazin (New York: World, 1951) pp. 72–7

Schlesinger, Arthur, Jr., *The Crisis of the Old Order* (Boston: Houghton Mifflin, 1957)

Sklar, Robert, *F. Scott Fitzgerald: The Last Laocoön* (New York: Oxford University Press, 1967)

Steinberg, Abraham H., "Fitzgerald's Portrait of a Psychiatrist", in *Tender is the Night: Essays in Criticism*, ed. Marvin J. LaHood (Bloomington: Indiana University Press, 1969) pp. 138–43

Stern, Milton R., *The Golden Moment: The Novels of F. Scott Fitzgerald* (Urbana: University of Illinois Press, 1970)

Tomkins, Calvin, *Living Well is the Best Revenge* (New York: Viking, 1971)

Trilling, Lionel, "F. Scott Fitzgerald", in *F. Scott Fitzgerald: The Man and His Work*, ed. Alfred Kazin (New York: World, 1951) pp. 195–205

Troy, William, "Scott Fitzgerald—The Authority of Failure", in *F. Scott Fitzgerald: A Collection of Critical Essays*, ed. Arthur M. Mizener (Englewood Cliffs, N.J.: Prentice-Hall, 1963) pp. 188–94

Tuchman, Barbara, *The Guns of August* (New York: Macmillan, 1962)

Turnbull, Andrew, *Scott Fitzgerald* (New York: Scribner's, 1962)

Westcott, Glenway, "The Moral of Scott Fitzgerald", in *The Crack-Up*, ed. Edmund Wilson (New York: New Directions, 1945) pp. 323–37

Woodress, James, ed., *American Literary Scholarship* (Durham, N.C.: Duke University Press, 1965–75)

Index